Jan. 7, 2022

Stephanie,

It was great meeting you over lunch in Jackson Hole, and I'm enjoying and appreciating your smart, insightful "Dear Diary" political commentary emails.

Julie's already talking about a return trip together to Wyoming. Yea!

I hope you enjoy Zeb's a book. I look forward to seeing you again!

A Place at the Table

A Place at the Table

*The true story of two men—
best friends in their youth,
reunited in adversity*

Alan Stoudemire

CHEROKEE PUBLISHING COMPANY
Atlanta, Georgia
2002

Library of Congress Cataloging-in-Publication Data

Stoudemire, Alan.
A place at the table: The true story of two men—best friends in their youth, reunited in adversity
p. cm.
ISBN 0-87797 286-9
1. Stoudemire, Alan--Childhood and youth. 2. Blake, Boyce--Childhood and youth. 3. Lincolnton (N.C.)--Biography. 4. Friendship--North Carolina--Lincolnton. 5. Afro-American men--North Carolina--Lincolnton--Biography. 6. White men--North Carolina--Lincolnton-- Biography. 7. Lincolnton (N.C.)--Race relations. I. Title.
F264.L55 S76 2000
975.6'782--dc21
[B]   99-049019

Manufactured in the United States of America

ISBN: 0-87797-286-9

06 05 04 03 02   10 9 8 7 6 5 4 3 2 1

Edited by Alexa Selph
Designed by Kenneth W. Boyd

Cover photo by Robert Lahser, *The Charlotte Observer*
From a Distance Words and Music by Julie Gold
Copyright (c) 1986 Julie Gold Misic (BMI) and Wing & Wheel Music (BMI)
Julie Gold Music Administered Worldwide by Cherry River Music Co.
Wing & Wheel Music Administered by Irving Music, Inc.
International Copyright Secured All Rights Reserved Used by permission

 CHEROKEE PUBLISHING COMPANY
P.O. Box 1730, Marietta, GA 30061

DEDICATION

To the memory of three of my friends:
Sergeant Paul "Skip" Lawing,
United States Army Special Forces,
killed in action in Vietnam,
June 14, 1972, at the age of twenty-one;
Captain Jeb Seagle,
United States Marine Corps helicopter pilot,
killed in action in Grenada,
October 25, 1983, at the age of thirty;
and especially to
Boyce Blake and his family

CONTENTS

ACKNOWLEDGMENTS

I wish to acknowledge the support and faith in my work of a number of individuals who made the telling of this story possible. Donna "Punkin" Blake Tolliver represented the Blake family and provided me with access to family records and traditions that were essential to the story. United States Senator Max Cleland was a tireless friend and a constant source of inspiration. Joe DePriest of the *Charlotte Observer* should be given all the credit for recognizing the significance of the story of the friendship between Boyce Blake and me. Ken Boyd of Cherokee Publishing Company revived this project when prospects for completing it seemed bleak. Ken spent countless hours in field-level background research on the history of Lincoln County and its people.

Darrell Harkey, head of the Lincoln County Historical Commission, fully devoted his time in a selfless way to provide me, my editors, and publisher with information that would otherwise have been impossible to obtain. His assistance not only enriched this story but made it possible to tell it in a historically authentic manner. He was also a critical source for many of the historic photographs of the early days of the county. My sister, Sylvia Stoudemire Wallace, proved to be of invaluable help, gathering much-needed family history. Rudolph Young made available his invaluable genealogical research on the African American families and history of slavery in Lincoln County and furnished information regarding the Blake family. Sheriff Harvin Crouse and Sheriff Barbara Pickens provided long-lost stories of the Lincoln County moonshiners and the techniques of their trade. Deputy Sheriff Earline Johnson gave me more recent information regarding the history of integration in Lincoln County and the history of Newbold High School, the only all-black high school in Lincoln County, which closed in 1968.

My editors, Lucy Emerson Sullivan and Alexa Selph, enabled me to make the difficult transition from scientific writing to telling this story in published form, displaying remarkable patience in the process.

I would like to thank the descendants of Victor Fair for making available the writings and historical records of Victor Fair, a descendant of Christian Reinhardt, who owned the Revolutionary War era tannery near Ramsour's Mill on the outskirts of the town of Lincolnton in and around where the Battle of Ramsour's Mill took place in 1780.

I would like to thank Shannon and Dan Amos of Columbus, Georgia, for their generous support and faith in my work.

Finally, I want to thank my wife, Sue, who has always believed in and encouraged me, who has helped with each step of this project, and who is the person who most sustained me in completing this book amidst multiple life traumas.

PROLOGUE

Only one soldier under the command of George Armstrong Custer was still alive after the Battle of Little Bighorn, when the Sioux Indians attacked the United States Cavalry in 1876. In 1871, this same Troop C of the Seventh United States Cavalry Regiment, whose destiny lay in wait for them by the Little Bighorn Creek in the Dakota territory, was sent to Lincolnton, North Carolina, to restore order after members of the Ku Klux Klan had covertly taken over control of the county government. Troop C was housed in the North State Hotel, which stood intact until it was demolished in 1968. While the troop was housed in the hotel, Daniel Alexander Kanipe joined this cavalry unit. Once order was restored, Troop C departed Lincolnton in 1872 and was sent to the Western territories in 1875 to participate in the wars against the Plains Indians in the Black Hills of the Dakotas. Several days before the attack of Chiefs Sitting Bull, Crazy Horse, and Rain-in-the-Face, Custer sent Corporal Kanipe for reinforcements. We all know what Kanipe found when he returned.

I grew up with distant descendants of Daniel Kanipe, like Milton and Dana Kanipe. I personally have nothing in common with Corporal Kanipe other than the fact that we both ate at the old North State Hotel by the Lincoln County Courthouse Square, we both stared at members of the Ku Klux Klan over a century apart at the exact same place, and we both managed to escape the odds arrayed against us long enough to tell our stories.

∞∞

Over 120 years later, in October of 1997, I found myself again in Lincolnton after many years away. It was near midnight, and almost everyone had drifted away from the funeral home. I was alone at the street edge of the mortuary's parking lot, when a tall black man slowly moved up behind me until we stood shoulder to shoulder. Well aware of each other's presence, we did not speak at first but stared into the night. The town was now quiet, but not unusually so for a small North Carolina town of about ten thousand people.

Directly across the street from us was an old elementary school that had once housed the county library. It now served as the Lincoln County Sheriff's Department, complete with a small jail for detaining prisoners.

The Sheriff's Department currently in the old brick building held the distinction of having Barbara Pickens serve as sheriff. Sheriff Pickens was the first female elected sheriff in the history of North Carolina. She had worked at the old sheriff's office as a dispatcher ever since she was a teenager, and she gradually grew into her role as a candidate for elected office. I had known Barbara and her younger brother Herbert, whom we called affectionately "Baby Hubby" when he was a child. We had grown up together in the local Lutheran Church not far from where we stood that night.

Diagonally across the street was an old two-story building made of red clay brick. I knew its history well. Built in 1817, it had housed a private school for the wealthier boys of the town and had been called the Pleasant Retreat Academy. It had produced three Confederate generals, Robert Hoke, Robert Johnston, and Stephen Dodson Ramseur, and James Pinckney Henderson, the first governor of the state of Texas. By the early 1900s the Academy building had been converted into the county's only library. The old building with ivy desperately clutching at its sides was now the home of the Daughters and Sons of the Confederacy, with a Confederate Museum housed on the second floor.

We remained there together for a few more seconds of silence. We both seemed to be looking in the direction of the old memorial to the Confederacy. The black man beside me spoke first.

"Your mama used to work at that old place when we were little, didn't she?"

"Yeah, she did, until they moved the library across the street to the old grammar school and then to the new library up on Main Street. I spent a lot of time there waiting for her to close up and take us home. I haven't been inside for thirty years. It probably hasn't changed a bit."

The black man responded quickly and tensely as if talk about the library had irritated him. "Well, there's one thing that has changed. They'll let black folk check out books now from the new library. I bet you didn't know that they didn't used to let black kids check out books. The black teachers could, but not the kids."

Feeling defensive about my mother, as if she was being accused in some way, I came back at him quickly, "That was a long time before my mother ever worked there, and I never noticed her ever turning anybody away." Our conversation was taking an unpleasant turn, and I wanted it to end.

"There were a lot of things white folks didn't notice back in those days, or else they noticed and didn't care one way or the other. It was mostly the way they wanted it, like blacks having to sit in the balcony at the picture show where you couldn't hardly see the movie. Hell, they wouldn't even let us in the drive-in movies. And the swimming pools, forget it. You know better than anybody, Zeke. If it wasn't for us all damming up the creek, we wouldn't have had any place to swim."

I was glad he had called me by my nickname, which almost at once relieved the tension between us. The mention of our creek swimming pools brought smiles to both our faces.

"Yeah, we had some good times down on that old creek . . . and up on the hill in the church," I laughed.

Suddenly he laughed too, and I could tell that for both of us some of the old boyhood memories were coming back.

"Yeah, we had some good times. We'd had more fun if it hadn't been for that Punkin breakin' up our card games. And we'd got in a lot less trouble if it wasn't for Johnny. Johnny and Punkin, I tell you what, that was a pair . . . ," his voice trailed off softly, and I picked up the conversation.

"Makes you almost want to go back and do it all over again. I tell you what, we had some wild times." We both laughed, sharing slightly different, but mutually good, memories.

After a pause, he began again, "Yeah, we had some good times, but when you went off to college and they started drafting every black kid in Georgetown to go to 'Nam, that's when it all ended."

The mention of Vietnam cast a chill over the conversation that seemed to cool even the night air.

We stood in silence again, and I noticed it was almost one o'clock in the morning. The funeral home appeared locked down for the night, except for the chapel, where a few people were determined to remain at the wake all night long in front of the open steel casket surrounded by flowers.

Our boyhood memories began to flood my mind. I had been gone for almost thirty years. In some ways nothing had changed, and in other ways, everything had changed. I had come home again to this place of happiness and sadness, life and death, black and white.

This is a story about that little town and our lives in it. For a time, we managed to carve out a separate peace for ourselves in this small place in the foothills of the southern Appalachian Mountains. Some of us never left, and others would never come home again. I had come home again for just a little while, and we found ourselves in the quiet of that lonely night reliving our time there together.

Crossing the Creek

You must know that there is nothing
higher and stronger and more wholesome
and good for life in the future than some
good memory, especially a memory of
childhood, of home.

—Fyodor Dostoyevsky,
The Brothers Karamazov

Looking back on it now, I believe I was born of
two families: one white and the other black. The two
families were separated by a small stream that ran through
a small valley in the heavily forested foothills of my home
in North Carolina. The stream arose from a little spring
hidden in the thickets of my family farm and now resides
in the thickets of my memory.

If you looked out, as if from above, over the rolling
foothills of the Blue Ridge Mountains, you would find our
farm and, near it a little ways into the surrounding woods,

the stream. On one side, there was our family of five: my mother, my father, brother Stewart, sister Sylvia, and myself. Our mother was a direct descendant of Scottish mountain people, and our father of German Protestant immigrants going back almost three hundred years into the history of the Carolina wilderness. On the opposite side of that stream was a family of fourteen, descendants of African-born slaves.

Sometime around 1844, a passenger steamship traveled from Baltimore to Savannah, Georgia. In the hold of the ship were West Africans who had been kidnapped to be sold as slaves in America. They were first brought to port in Baltimore, Maryland. From there, a steamship would transport them to the slave market in Savannah, where the demand for slaves was high, due to Georgia's large cotton plantations. In transit, somewhere off the coast of Wilmington, North Carolina, a pregnant female slave went into labor. The captain made the decision to pull into port there so that the mother would be more likely to deliver her baby safely. If she were to die in labor, her cash value would obviously be lost and the baby would be likely to die, as well. On the other hand, if mother and baby both survived, the sale of the infant would provide a bonus. The mother delivered her male child safely on board ship. Mother, child, and father were bought at the Wilmington slave market by an Irishman named Dunovant, and the baby was named Charlie. Later separated from his family, Charlie was bought by an Englishman named Blake.

When I was a boy in the 1960s, my best friend was named Boyce Blake. The young African woman aboard the ship bound to Savannah was Boyce's great-great-grandmother. Her baby was Boyce's great-grandfather Charlie, who took the last name of his owner when he was freed in 1865. At the same time that Charlie Blake was released from the bondage of slavery, my great-grandfather Robert "Robin" Stewart, private, Confederate States of America, was walking home wounded to his mountain cabin somewhere deep in the southern Appalachian Mountains of the Carolinas.

Boyce's family lived on the other side of the creek from mine. The waters of the little creek that ran in a wooded valley between our two families eventually flowed into the South Fork of the Catawba River a few miles downstream. On my side of the creek, despite the beauty of the place, I was isolated and often unbearably lonely. My brother, Stewart McBryde Stoudemire, nine years my senior, left for college when I was only nine years old. After Stewart left, I had no companions to play with about the woods and hills of the farm. My sister, Sylvia, six years older than me, had little interest in the rough and ready life that lay beyond the sunny edges of our pastures, where, in the dark coolness of the woods, the mysteries and adventures of the forest began.

Sylvia spent most of her time reading when she was not helping my mother fry chicken, bake bread, or can for winter consumption the large variety of vegetables grown in our

BOYCE BLAKE'S FAMILY TREE

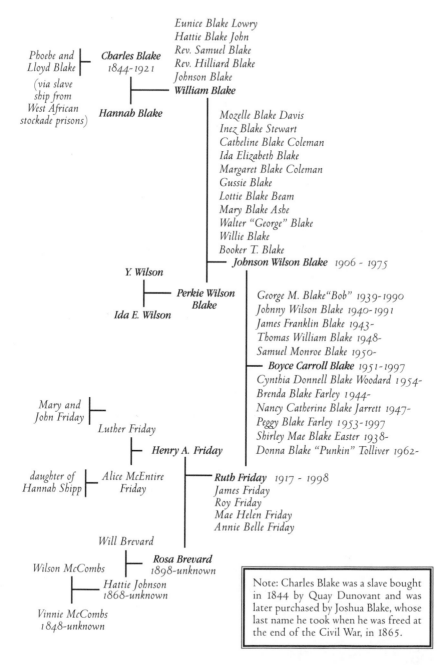

Phoebe and
Lloyd Blake
(via slave
ship from
West African
stockade prisons)

Charles Blake
1844-1921

Hannah Blake

Eunice Blake Lowry
Hattie Blake John
Rev. Samuel Blake
Rev. Hilliard Blake
Johnson Blake
William Blake

Mozelle Blake Davis
Inez Blake Stewart
Catheline Blake Coleman
Ida Elizabeth Blake
Margaret Blake Coleman
Gussie Blake
Lottie Blake Beam
Mary Blake Ashe
Walter "George" Blake
Willie Blake
Booker T. Blake
Johnson Wilson Blake *1906 - 1975*

Y. Wilson

Perkie Wilson Blake

Ida E. Wilson

George M. Blake "Bob" *1939-1990*
Johnny Wilson Blake *1940-1991*
James Franklin Blake *1943-*
Thomas William Blake *1948-*
Samuel Monroe Blake *1950-*
Boyce Carroll Blake *1951-1997*
Cynthia Donnell Blake Woodard *1954-*
Brenda Blake Farley *1944-*
Nancy Catherine Blake Jarrett *1947-*
Peggy Blake Farley *1953-1997*
Shirley Mae Blake Easter *1938-*
Donna Blake "Punkin" Tolliver *1962-*

Mary and
John Friday

Luther Friday

Henry A. Friday

daughter of
Hannah Shipp

Alice McEntire
Friday

Ruth Friday *1917 - 1998*
James Friday
Roy Friday
Mae Helen Friday
Annie Belle Friday

Will Brevard

Rosa Brevard
1898-unknown

Wilson McCombs

Hattie Johnson
1868-unknown

Vinnie McCombs
1848-unknown

Note: Charles Blake was a slave bought in 1844 by Quay Dunovant and was later purchased by Joshua Blake, whose last name he took when he was freed at the end of the Civil War, in 1865.

MR. CHARLES BLAKE.– OBITUARY.

By Rev. H. Blake.

Mr. Charles Blake died March 7th, 1921, in Chester, S.C. His funeral was preached by the Rev. R. A. McCrary, D. D., of Chester, S.C. His body was laid to rest in Gold Mine cemetery, beside his first wife, Mrs. Hannah Blake, who died 28 years ago. Mr. Blake was the son of Lloyd and Phoebe Blake, born in 1844, on the Atlantic Ocean, somewhere between the State of Maryland and Wilmington, N.C.

His land at Wilmington, N.C. was sold to Mr. Quay Dunovant. After the death of Mr. Dunovant, it was sold to Mr. Joshua Blake, near Bascomville, S. C. He spent the greater part of his life within twenty miles of the above named place. He was converted at Mt. Zion church in 1880. Lived a Christian life for nearly 40 years. Died in his 77th year. He leaves four sons and two daughters to survive him, namely: H. Blake, of Charlotte; W. M. Blake, of Lincolnton; Rev. S. Blake, of Richburg; S. C; Johnson Blake of Great Falls, S. C.; Miss Hattie Blake, of Rock Hill, S. C.; Mrs. Eunice Lowry, of Chester, S. C.

Rest in peace. We will see you again.

REPRINTED FROM THE "STAR OF ZION", MARCH, 1921. OBITUARY OF BOYCE BLAKE'S GREAT-GRANDFATHER, FORMER SLAVE, CHARLES BLAKE, WRITTEN BY HIS SON, REV. HILLIARD BLAKE.

huge garden. Her other principal job was to help my mother keep the house clean—not an easy task, because our cats and dogs were given free range of the place. The dogs learned how to open the back screen door by catching the wire with their paws and nosing the door open, so they wandered in and out of the house at will. There were the family dog Chip, my own dog Whitey, whom I had raised from a puppy, and a tabby cat we called Mr. Big. Mr. Big was a very large cat!

Sylvia must have been as painfully lonely as I was on this beautiful, but isolated land. We had little in common in those days other than a proclivity for reading. Aside from reading, the main things we shared were the farm duties dictated by our father and the strict discipline of our Scots-Irish mother.

My mother's family name was Stewart, a large Scottish clan that had settled in the southern Appalachians. With her family scattered about the southwestern Carolina mountains, details of the family tree were sketchy, but it is clear that my mother, Louise Stewart, was of direct Scottish descent. Her father, Oscar Sloan Stewart, was born in 1868, only three years after the Civil War ended. His father was Robert "Robin" Stewart, who had walked home from the battlefields of Virginia. My mother was only three months old when her mother, Hattie Johnston Stewart, died of heart failure at age forty. Six years later Papa Stewart remarried a Scots-Irish woman named Josie

Chastain to help raise my mother and her two sisters, all under ten at the time of their mother's death.

My father once told me that "Miss Josie" had been all but written off by family and community as an old maid until Oscar's marriage proposal to her. My father seemed to have held little fondness for my mother's stepmother. He claimed that Miss Josie married Papa Stewart in order to save social face and to guarantee her security in old age, but that she did not want children at that late stage in her life. She was described by my mother as a cold, strict, and distant stepmother who seemed to resent the unwanted burden of Oscar's children. The loss of her own mother and the coldness of Miss Josie left traces of sadness in my mother's personality. Death in the mountains came to these people in unexpected and untimely ways and could leave its cruel scars on a child for a lifetime. My mother managed to survive the loneliness of her childhood, and following several years of college, she married my father on Christmas Day 1940, less than a year before the Japanese attack on Pearl Harbor.

At the time of my parents' wedding, my father, George Stoudemire, was a recent graduate of Clemson College, which in those days was an all-male military college. He had managed to put himself through college by working in the hot, dusty, dangerous sawmills of the mid-Carolinas during the summer months. He came from a poor family of ten children, two of whom died in childhood. His father,

Asman, was foreman of a track repair crew for the Southern Railroad. His mother died of a brain tumor when he was only twelve years old. Thereafter, the children were raised by his oldest sister, Martha, or Mot, as she was called.

My father was well over six feet tall, broad-shouldered, tough-skinned, strong, affable, and a devoted and faithful husband. He compensated my mother in part for the love she had missed as a child. My mother frequently referred to him as her best friend. Shortly after their marriage, however, he was sent off to the Pacific in World War II, along with many other of the 1941 graduates of Clemson College. He was commissioned as a second lieutenant in the United States Army and rapidly promoted to captain.

After pursuing the Japanese from island to island in the Philippines with his tank company, my father came home when the war ended. Shortly after I was born, my parents moved to the farm outside the small rural town of Lincolnton, the only home that I remember.

You could reach our farm from two different directions. One way was to turn off the main southbound road leading out of Lincolnton onto Victory Grove Church Road. If you then took a left turn just before you reached the Victory Grove Church itself, you would find yourself on Jerry Crump Road, at one of the highest elevations in Lincoln County. The expansive view to the southwest provided the first glimpse of our farm and some of the town's more prominent church steeples scattered amidst the distant trees. Beyond that lay the south range of the Blue Ridge Mountains. A little further down the road, a turn onto an even smaller dirt road ended a half-mile beyond at our farm.

The other way to reach the farm was the northerly route from the other end of Jerry Crump Road. The road was named for Jerry Crump, a local hero who was one of Lincoln County's three Medal of Honor winners. As a young man of seventeen, Corporal Crump threw himself on top of a live North Korean grenade to protect four wounded comrades by covering the explosive with his body and absorbing its hot shrapnel. Remarkably, Corporal Crump survived the grenade blast. On the night of January 10, 1977, he was returning from a meeting of the Veterans of Foreign Wars when his truck skidded off the road and burst into flames. After all he had endured in Korea, Jerry Crump was dead alongside an isolated road in rural Lincoln County at age forty-three.

After turning onto Jerry Crump Road, you would see atop an elegantly landscaped hill an imposing, two-story, frame building with large, white columns. Out front flew a large American flag, and situated near it stood an old, rusted anti-aircraft cannon. This was the clubhouse of Lincoln County's chapter of the Veterans of Foreign Wars, commonly referred to as the VFW. Beside it was the VFW's private "members only" swimming pool. Directly across the road on another hill was the small, white home of Berl Plonck, a well-known local bootlegger.

After passing Berl's house, you crossed a small wooden bridge over a large stream that originated from a spring about a mile away. This spring was famous in the nineteenth century for the high concentration of lithium salts its water contained. These salts were believed to be therapeutic for a variety of maladies. The locally famous Lithia Springs Inn, a large, sprawling hotel, was built near the spring, so that well-to-do travelers could come and enjoy drinking and bathing in the health-giving waters. After the Civil War, Confederate General Robert F. Hoke, reputed to be General Lee's replacement if Lee was killed during the war, bought the inn and spring and retired there. It was here at the Lithia Springs Inn that General Hoke would talk for hours about his days serving under his friend Robert E. Lee.

Having passed the stream, you would begin the climb up what we called Bootleg Hill, a dirt road that had to be driven with great care at night. On more than one occasion, we would encounter, sprawled out in the middle of the road, drunks who had passed out on their way back from a visit to Berl's before they could reach their wooden shacks set back in the shade of the woods along the road. Upon confronting one of these unfortunate souls, I recall my father saying, "Even a pig knows better than to sleep in the middle of the road." We would stop the car and blow the horn until the inebriate managed to rouse himself. My father was careful to keep our car lights on him until he had managed to stumble into the woods, so he would not be run over by another passing car, truck, or tractor. Once the drunk had found the relative safety of the woods, we would continue on our way home, leaving him to his own devices, which were usually adequate.

The other entrance to our farm property, by way of the Victory Grove Church Road, was the safer route, especially at night, but I personally preferred going by Berl Plonck's house and the VFW. You never knew who you might run into along the way home.

Once you had made the turn onto our little dirt road, you would see immediately the small, white frame homes of the only neighbors on our road: Hazel and Ernest Carpenter on one side, Lee and Lillian Armstrong on the other. Hazel and "Ern" worked in textile mills and maintained a large vegetable garden next to the road. They had one child, a daughter born when Hazel was nearly forty years old. The birth came as a surprise to everyone, as it was accepted that Ern and Hazel had given up on attempting to have children. Like the Carpenters and like many other small farmers in Lincoln County, Lee and Lillian had to take textile mill jobs to make ends meet, and they did their farming on the side.

Just past the Carpenters' and Armstrongs' on the right was a relatively small forest of white pine trees that covered about five acres. I vividly recall the day when, as a boy, I held in my hand clumps of small pine seedlings, as I helped my father plant hundreds of them, one by one. White pines grow fast in the South, reaching maturity in thirty years or less. Our stand of trees grew into a beautiful, little shaded forest where rabbits and squirrels scurried back and forth from a nearby spring.

After passing the pines, you would reach the crest of another hill, one of the highest elevations in the county, where our farmland would suddenly rise before you and be dramatically laid out with the outline of the south range of the Blue Ridge Mountains in the far distance. Our house, yard, well house, and barn lay straight ahead. These buildings were encircled by gently down-sloping pastureland, then surrounded by a dense, hardwood forest. Through this forest was visible a single church steeple, and beyond that, the mountains in the distance. At this point, barbed-wire fence, which enclosed our pastures, lined the road on either side, along with scattered shade trees. The small farm's three pastures were used alternately for growing corn, wheat, oats, and barley, then rotated and put back into pasture for the animals.

In the middle of the three large pasture areas was our simple, white, one-story wooden house. Originally built around 1900, various additions, including two bedrooms, had been made over the years. Directly in front of the house, adjacent to our open, covered porch, was a huge red maple tree at least two hundred feet tall with a circumference of ten to twelve feet. My father estimated it to be pre-Revolutionary and, therefore, at least two hundred years old. Besides providing welcome shade and beauty for our home and my family, it was a wonderful climbing tree. I spent the better part of my childhood in treehouses my brother, Stewart, and I built in its strong arms, which never let us down.

A small brick building we called the well house lay ten feet from the main house at the opposite end of the small porch. It enclosed an old dry hand-dug well and my mother's washing machine. It also served as the storehouse for the beans, tomatoes, pickled cucumbers, jellies and jams, and multiple other vegetables and fruits she canned from the huge family garden. Beyond the well house, screened by a row of dense, unhewn hedges—sometimes reaching twelve feet high—was an old red horse barn. A small opening in the hedge provided a pathway between the house and barn. With a tin roof, the barn consisted of a series of stables and larger areas where hay was stored. Behind the barn stood a small shed we simply called the "red house," which was used for storing oats and corn for the animals in the winter. It provided one corner of the hog pen, actually a small pasture where our lucky porkers could stroll and root about as they pleased and enjoy summertime naps in the cool shade offered by the stand of trees at the periphery of their enclosure. In bad weather, they slept piled on top of each other underneath the red house.

Two areas of the farm were a special source of pride for my parents. My mother's large flower garden covered almost half an acre of land, and additional flowers were scattered about the lawn surrounding the house. Friends and even strangers would come by the house unannounced on Sunday afternoons in the spring just to see "Miss Lou's" flowers. Whether it was to see my mother's flowers or not, dropping by to visit family or friends completely unannounced was a common custom in the South. Sometimes on Sunday afternoons, the driveway in our yard would hold seven or eight cars at any given time. In good weather, we would bring chairs from the house and sit beneath the old maple tree or in the swing on the porch. We would listen while the grownups sat and talked for hours, drinking heavily sweetened iced tea with lemon.

Often the talk would be about my father's vineyard. It was his pride and joy and one of his obsessions. Wild muscadine grapes were indigenous to the region, and my father had well over eighty separate vines and nineteen varieties of the hardy native grapes. The vineyard was beautiful, but for me, its sight only signified the endless hours of mowing the surrounding grass and the laborious hours of pruning its vines.

A barbed-wire fence separated the lawn encircling the house from the pasture and other fields. In various places around the lawn there were fruit trees of almost every variety, including several cherry trees, two pear trees, a plum tree that grew productively over our septic tank, an apple tree, and at one time, a peach tree that did not survive the altitude. I had helped my father plant three pecan trees that grew to be huge and highly productive. Sometimes in full season, the limbs of the trees would break under the strain of its weighty yield of pecans.

There was a persimmon tree beside the barn. Unlike the Cherokee Indians, to whom the land once belonged, we made no use of the tree's acerbic fruit. The Cherokee knew how to make bread out of persimmons.

A short distance from the house and over one fence, you entered the woods that separated our property from that of the Blakes. As you entered the forest and walked down a gentle hill, a small creek that ran through a valley would come into view. Once you reached the stream, you were out of sight of all civilization.

Along the banks of the creek were mysterious holes that were the homes of cottonmouth water moccasins, whose startling appearance would send us scattering. Perhaps the most terrifying sight of my youth was that of a moccasin suddenly emerging from the water with a hapless frog clenched within its fangs and white jaws. I would run to get my rifle or shotgun to fend off the monster and attempt a heroic frog rescue. Of course, by the time I had made the trip up through the wooded hill across our fenced pasture, opened and closed the gate to keep our cows from escaping, run across our front yard and into our house, and then made the return trip to the creek, the snake had long since slithered beneath the water's surface back into its hiding place to devour and enjoy the frog, legs and all. The snakes of our creek seemed to thrive. Although the creek banks must still be full of empty shotgun shells, I have no recollection of ever having actually killed a snake.

Even in this paradise of barn and fields and woods and creek and animals, my brother, Stewart, needed more to keep himself amused, and so he put his genius to work on various barnyard inventions. I was often his guinea pig. One such brainstorm resulted in a rotating Ferris wheel made of old boards that were nailed together. The rickety structure was an amazing forty feet from the ground to the top and quite dangerous, if anyone had bothered to think seriously about it. For us, it was wonderfully thrilling. Upon its completion, Stewart charged us each a nickel to ride it, while he turned it by hand, propelling us skyward.

He also built a wooden merry-go-round, which could best be described as an octagonal wooden wheel turned on its side and mounted on a post so that it could rotate. We would sit on the edges of the wooden wheel and hold on for dear life. Stewart would take great delight in spinning us around so fast that we would become nauseated and beg him to stop and let us off. These pleas generally served to incite him to spin us faster. If we were lucky, our mother would hear our screams for mercy, order Stewart to stop, and make him promise always to stop when we asked. Of course, he promised to do so. Eventually, we would beg him to "give us a spin" again, and the entire cycle would repeat itself. Stewart was less than predictable and even less trustworthy under such circumstances, which added to the excitement of the barnyard circus.

Another attraction at this carnival was our infamous "kamikaze run" off the barn's tin roof (called "kamikaze" for the suicidal Japanese airmen our father told us about, who would intentionally crash their bomb-loaded planes into American ships during the war). Stewart had found a large baby carriage that had probably been used for me. It became the suicidal vehicle of descent from the barn roof. First, he would pile a large stack of hay at the base of the barn. Then the carriage would be positioned and held at the pinnacle of the barn's roof, and into it either Sylvia, I, or sometimes Stewart himself was crammed. Finally, the carriage was released, and the screaming occupant would fly down the side of the roof and eventually careen into the air for the twenty-foot drop into the hay. By some miracle, we always emerged with spine and neurological functioning intact. The kamikaze operation ended when our horrified mother discovered it. After that, Stewart made plenty of rope swings and other substitute diversions that were somewhat safer, but less thrilling, aerial rides. Our father seemed to ignore these antics as long as we didn't use any "good" boards he was saving for one of his serious construction projects and as long as our activities did not cut into our work time on the farm.

My brother also made a go-cart, a small jerry-rigged race car equipped with an old lawn mower motor mounted on its side so that its heavy black fan belt could be hooked up to an axle between the wheels. The wheels were held together by a hollow iron pipe about three feet long. The base of the go-cart was made of wood, and the magical machine was guided with ropes connected to either side of the front wheels. Stewart's most advanced model actually had a steering wheel with ropes from the front axle wrapped about a steel pipe steering pole. An old bicycle wheel was used to turn the front wheels.

Given the materials available to him, Stewart's go-carts were rather remarkable feats of backyard engineering. After he left for college, the farm circus fell into disrepair, and the go-cart gradually fell apart. The fun on my side of the creek all but ended with Stewart's departure.

The little creek that ran between our property and the Blakes' took a serpentine path through the small, shaded valley among the trees of the forest, which provided a canopy where gentle light came and went with the passing of clouds, the passing of days and nights, and the gentle passing of my boyhood. Birds of almost every kind found water there, along with the occasional squirrel and rabbit that came for a drink.

There were cardinals, hawks, quail, doves, sparrows, wrens, screech owls, blue jays, whippoorwills, mockingbirds, swallows, robins, crows, and sometimes red-headed woodpeckers that visited our creek. Foxes lived in the area, but they were rarely seen, earning their reputation for stealth and privacy. Possum, raccoons, and skunks were notorious for their epicurean raids on our trash cans. If a family of skunks decided to take up residence under the house, it was trouble for sure. They would not give up their territory, won many years before our family turned up on the scene, without a noxious fight.

On the opposite side of the stream about a quarter of a mile away through the woods, along another ridge of high ground lived my second family, Boyce Blake and his siblings and his parents. The balm for my loneliness was only one Tarzan call away through those woods to the Blake house.

When challenged by Boyce, I could rattle off the names of his siblings: brothers Sam, Tom, Johnny, Frank, and George (nicknamed "Bob" for some reason), and sisters Shirley, Peggy, Nancy, Cynthia, Brenda, and the youngest, Donna (nicknamed "Pumpkin," and affectionately called "Punkin" by everyone). Sometimes I would lose the bet to name them all, but the real challenge would be to get them in their correct birth order, a feat I never mastered.

Early on in our friendship, Johnny, one of Boyce's older brothers, had dubbed me "Zeke." No one seemed to know the derivation of this nickname. When I would ask him why he called me Zeke, Johnny would only laugh and say, "'Cause you just look like a 'Zeke' to me!" I appreciate now that being given a nickname was an honor on Blake Hill, as it signified acceptance into their relatively small but elite circle of brotherhood and friendship.

Years later, Tom came up with what I consider the best theory for the origin of the name. Tom was reasonably sure that Johnny's inspiration was a cartoon character in their old grammar school *Weekly Reader:* Zeke the Janitor. Whatever the origin, the nickname would follow me into high school, college, medical school, residency training, and even professional life. My wife would never call me by any other name.

Boyce's name was chosen to honor the doctor who delivered him: Dr. Boyce Griggs. Because Dr. Griggs was one of only a few general practitioners in the area who would deliver black babies in the early 1950s, the name Boyce was not uncommon among the young black males of Lincolnton. Boyce had been given the nickname Fox by his brothers and sisters. I never knew the origin of his nickname, but it seemed to refer to his stealthy way of moving about, the sly grin that was often on his face, and his uncanny ability to stay out of trouble.

Boyce's parents were only one generation removed from slavery, and yet I never heard them talk of any generation other than their own. A local black historian and genealogist by the name of Rudolph Young, however, had researched and compiled information on a number of black families in the area and had traced some of them back to slave days. One of those families was Boyce Blake's.

Boyce's great-grandfather Charlie had a son named Hilliard who became a minister in the newly organized all-black African Methodist Episcopal Zion Church (the A.M.E. Church). Reverend Hilliard Blake was sent by A.M.E. Zion Church officials to neighboring Gaston County, divided from Lincoln County by the South Fork River, and he assumed his duties there. In the 1920s, he crossed the old bridge over the South Fork River at the mill village of Flat Shoals to pastor the locally prestigious African Methodist Episcopal Church in Lincolnton.

Reverend Hilliard Blake's brother William, another son of the former slave Charlie, moved with him to the area. William Blake was Boyce's grandfather. He raised twelve children with his wife Perkie Wilson Blake, and one of their sons was named Johnson. Johnson Blake was to become Boyce's father. Another son of William Blake was the Reverend Samuel Blake.

Johnson Blake married Ruth Friday, whose family came from the eastern part of the county near a little community alternately called Ironton or Iron Station, where slaves once were used to run huge stone furnaces that made iron implements and cannonballs for the Confederacy. Confederate trains stopped at Iron Station, and slaves would load its railroad cars with iron cannonballs meant to kill Yankee soldiers. Eventually, the track was destroyed by the Yankee soldiers who poured into the Carolinas from northwest Virginia near the end of the war. The iron industry there faded into history, and the black families gradually dispersed from the area.

Boyce's father, Johnson Blake, had earned a Bronze Star for his service in the Pacific war theater in World War II. He held the distinction of being one of the first black men to have been allowed to work in one of the local cotton mills following the war. He had worked at the Long Shoals mill for over twenty-five years. He had held his large family of twelve children together and enjoyed the prestige of having a church on his own property.

Life was hard for the Blakes, but the family was tough. I never heard them complain. During this time, the Blakes had to haul water from the well next to their house, bucket by bucket, for every conceivable household purpose, from cooking to washing clothes to bathing. Several huge black cast-iron pots positioned about the yard were filled with water and heated by wood fires for washing and boiling clothes. Baths were taken in a special room that contained an oil stove. The house was heated by a combination of wood and oil stoves scattered about the rambling, unpainted wooden structure. There were six bedrooms for the children who were still at home, segregated by gender, of course, and the parents' bedroom. The interior of the house was clean, but the wooden furniture was old, and porous cracks in the ceilings allowed several of the family cats to take up residence in the attic. Due to the vigilance of these attic dwellers, the house was at least free of mice. The Blakes never had a family dog, as I recall. A dog would have presented a problem for the "free range" chickens that pecked about the yard and under and around the house and church.

A common outhouse served as the only toilet for the family until around 1966, when one of the older brothers installed inside toilets and a septic tank. All of the laundry was done by hand. Chopping wood for the stoves was a task relegated to the men of the family.

Johnson Blake's wife, Ruth, was the indomitable matriarch of the family. She probably knew me as well as, if not better than, my own mother. "Miss Ruth" always seemed glad to see me. On weekends and throughout the summers, I became a fixture in the Blake household. If we were not playing cards or softball, we would be watching that week's professional football or basketball game on television.

Once my wife asked Miss Ruth what she had thought of Boyce and me while we were growing up. She remained quiet a few moments, then responded, "Two little devils! That's what they were. . . . Those boys were somethin' else runnin' up and down that creek!" When my wife went on to ask her what was the worst thing we ever did, however, she simply answered, "Well, they were never *that* bad I don't reckon!"

Besides Miss Ruth's ritualistic ranting and raving at some of our clandestine activities, which would inspire more laughter than fear in her children and in me, she was never critical. Miss Ruth bore no grudges after she had had her say on a subject. She ultimately seemed to forgive anything we could possibly do.

The sneaking of cigarettes and the occasional can of bootlegged beer and sip of moonshine was another matter in the court of Miss Ruth; all of us knew we would be in serious trouble if she ever found out we were smoking cigarettes or drinking anything stronger than a Coca-Cola. She never seemed to mind how late we played softball in the pasture or how long we stayed down at the creek. In fact, she seemed to enjoy watching us just having fun.

For the Blakes, I think, fun was more than just enjoying oneself; it was a matter of psychological survival, an escape from poverty and deprivation in a rural society, which kept them as members of an isolated, segregated underclass.

One overtly visible icon of segregation was the Veterans of Foreign Wars swimming pool, which had a sign that read "Members Only." My house was less than a mile from the VFW pool if you took the route through the woods past several pastures, over a few barbed-wire fences, across two creeks, and through the fields of the farm of our adjacent neighbor, Mr. Roberts. But I could never go swimming there with Boyce. In those days, "Members Only" was synonymous with "White Only."

The VFW officials would then, and still today, adamantly deny that club membership or the pool was open only to whites. The VFW officials claimed it was a "private" pool for members of the VFW and their families. No questions ever were asked of whites who came to swim there, but the few blacks who had on rare occasions bravely attempted to gain admittance to the pool were turned away because they were "not members." I never knew if any black veterans like Boyce's father had ever tried to join the VFW. As with so many other aspects of segregation, there were unwritten, but well-known rules. Every aspect of life was segregated at that time: eating, drinking, toilets, transportation, and education, as well as Christian worship. Segregation did not end even with death, as there were separate black and white cemeteries in town.

Amidst those years of segregation, the Blake family nevertheless carved out a small but lively world for themselves atop what was locally known as Blake Hill. I loved the free and sometimes lusty humor of Boyce and his brothers. What was considered "bad" then seems by comparison so innocent now. The relationship between our two families was centered primarily on the friendship between Boyce and me.

I have no precise memory of when I first met Boyce other than one afternoon I vaguely recall being drawn irresistibly to the noisy fun and shouts of one of their late spring softball games. I remember nervously crossing the creek and making the short hike up the wooded hill to the scrub pasture they used for a playing field. I wandered to the back edge of the field and found myself slowly gravitating toward Boyce, as we were about the same size, and I thought I might catch his eye for a brief second. I remember his saying something like "Hey, man! What are you doin'?" that seemed to call for a response from me.

"Y'all got room for another player?" I asked. I remember my anxiety over being rejected more than the words I sputtered out. I saw Boyce reach down for a bat and turn toward me as a grin broke out over his face, and he said, "You know how to use one of these things? Hang around awhile an' we'll find a place for you. It depends on who else shows up from down the road. What'd you say your name was? You from the other side of the hill?" I vaguely remember being put into the game after a short wait, as some players "from down the road" in the lower part of Georgetown didn't show up. I was a weak and unproven, but ready, reserve. I attracted no undue notice and was soon learning names and positions.

We were about ten years old at the time, and I remember that we hit it off almost at once. We were soon ready companions scouring the hot fields and cooler woods for blackberries that we would eat after carefully picking them from their thorny bushes. We tried to keep enough to take home to our mothers for blackberry pies.

When Boyce would emerge from the woods with a bucket of blackberries, he would be given something akin to a hero's welcome by the other Blake siblings because they knew it meant that Miss Ruth would have enough berries for a hot pie to be shared by the whole family. The other Blakes could appreciate, too, what it took to obtain enough black-berries to make a pie. Sometimes hours of hunting were involved in searching for a patch of blackberries that were in season. More hours were spent plucking the berries out of the dangerously thorny bushes, which did not give up their fruit willingly. Every now and then, we would be startled by a poisonous copperhead, which would rear its head and flash its menacing forked tongue at us to indicate its irritation at being disturbed. The snake always slithered silently away to find a more peaceful place to bask in the sun, leaving us shaken and anxious to move on to another part of the woods ourselves. Blackberry picking involved a small degree of dan-ger, which made our expeditions to find them more exciting.

Sometimes I ate all the blackberries I picked as we went along. They were irresistible. If I came home with an empty bucket, I could claim we hadn't found any that day, a small lie that was believable enough. The fact that Boyce managed to restrain himself from eating all of the berries on the spot I considered an act of admirable self-control. There is almost no better taste imaginable than a hot blackberry pie covered with vanilla ice cream, one made with berries that only a few hours earlier had been growing in the briar patches of their native fields, guarded by their patron snakes.

Among and around the blackberry bushes grew another plant of the forest not as healthy and wholesome as the blackberry bush. It was a grayish weed we called rabbit tobacco. No one was quite sure what rabbit tobacco was, but it was reputed to be what the Cherokee Indians of the area once smoked. The real tobacco weed would not grow high in the cool climate of the hills in western North Carolina. The fact that Cherokee Indians had once lived in the area in years past was confirmed by the arrowheads my father's plow occasionally turned up in our fields.

Rabbit tobacco's grayish weed seemed to thrive best amidst briar patches so that securing a sufficient supply of it to smoke was quite challenging. When the gray leaves were dried in the sun, they could be crushed and rolled into newspaper or stuffed into a pipe made of a hollowed-out corncob with a short stick of small cane inserted into the bottom. The noxious smoke was too acrid to be inhaled, so lighting up rabbit tobacco was primarily intended for the ritualistic purpose of imitating adults smoking real cigarettes. As far as I was concerned, smoking rabbit tobacco was good training for "real" smoking when a cigarette could be stolen from one of my father's open packs of filterless Camels.

Boyce, on the other hand, did not smoke rabbit tobacco or Camels, in spite of my efforts to get him to join me in a smoke. He had heard that smoking would "take your wind away," decrease your ability to play ball and to run, and might even stunt your growth. He would chide me for smoking "those cancer sticks." "You're crazy, man," he'd say. "Not only are you going to get cancer, but you're going to be a midget with cancer." Boyce had made the common-sense connection between smoking and lung cancer years before the United States Surgeon General gave his report on the subject. Sam was my usual smoking companion, but Sam, too, eventually declined to have anything to do with the foul-smelling weed.

As the two of us played along the creek, Boyce, or "Fox" as I came to call him back then, would often leave me there for a ball game with his black neighbors from the surrounding rural black community of Georgetown. They played in the pasture beside the Blake house next to the small Holiness Church that was on the Blake property.

The nature of the ball game would depend on the time of the year. When the pasture was not too muddy, they would play softball from late March through the end of October. The season for tag football, which could easily degenerate into hard blocks and "illegal" rough tackles, usually ran from sometime in October until the cold and wet weather of early December. In winter, basketball games were played on a small, hard, mud-packed court, which had a perimeter of no more than twenty feet and only one goal, usually nailed to a power line post or a tree. Finding a backboard was a problem solved by using the wooden headboard of an old bed we found on the edge of the woods.

So, whatever the season, a game would be going on almost every afternoon at the Blakes'. I would hear through the woods the shouts of laughter and giddy excitement and occasionally the sounds of heated disputes over a controversial call. Around the age of twelve, I felt that with Fox as my emissary, I was finally big enough to compete with the older black teenagers and a few in their early twenties, who dominated the field of play. I knew my participation depended solely on Fox's recommendation and also on the occasional need for an extra player. I was almost always on the reserve list whenever a big Georgetown weekend game was anticipated. When sides were chosen by the team captains, one of whom was always an older brother of Boyce's, I was usually the last player selected. There was no racial discrimination; I was simply the worst player on the field. As the years passed, and with the coaching of Boyce and his brothers, my skills became somewhat more respectable. I took pride in the fact that I moved up slightly on the pasture-ball draft list.

Weekend ball games could be played only on Saturday, as Miss Ruth forbade playing ball on Sunday. What she did not know, or pretended not to know, was that we had other activities planned for Sunday afternoons after church services.

Boyce's sister Punkin possessed a small inborn radar that could readily locate our whereabouts. She always seemed to have the ability to track us to the church, our favorite hiding place on cold, wet Sunday afternoons, even when she was a little girl of four. Fox and I and the other brothers were not gathered for prayer services, and Punkin somehow knew it.

The church on the Blake property had outgrown the small prayer meetings originally held in the rambling, unpainted, wooden Blake house, one of the largest homes in the black enclave of Georgetown. Shortly after Johnson Blake had returned from World War II, he and several of his neighbors, members of a home prayer group who met at the Blake house, built a "real" church on the edge of his three-acre plot. It was situated beside the ball field pasture and adjacent to a pen at times inhabited by several hogs the Blakes raised for butchering.

The one-room, tar paper-covered Holiness church had a wooden table and chairs at first. Later, used pews were donated by a fellow black church. It seated perhaps sixty worshippers at most and was heated with a simple stove fed by wood that was split on the Blake property. A makeshift table draped with a white linen cloth served as the altar, and a highly polished wooden oak cross was set upon it. A few worn brass collection plates for the Sunday offering could be found nearby.

Music was provided by several tambourines and a large, old bass drum donated by the local black high school, Newbold High. The bass drum kept the beat going for the gospel music and offered an occasional emphatic thump of approval when the local lay preacher made a particularly good spiritual point, which was also accompanied by cries of "Amen," "Yes, Brother," "Praise the Lord," or "Thank you, Jesus." On Sunday nights, I often heard the sound of the bass drum and the tambourines drifting through the woods, the impassioned and frenzied preaching of the lay minister, and the chant-like, soulful singing of the small but ecstatic congregation. Sometimes I became so fascinated that I would sneak through the woods and over the creek to the edge of the pasture to hear the singing better. The Blakes were continuing the family tradition of preaching and singing the Good News of Jesus, a tradition begun by Boyce's long-dead great-uncles, the Reverends Hilliard and Samuel Blake.

I knew little of the Blakes' Holiness Church's theology, except that the preacher's message was a pure and simple Jesus-centered one to repent, forgive, love your neighbor, and trust in Jesus's promise for a better life in the hereafter. The church was more than a place of worship; it was the heart of the Georgetown community, where most of the thirty or so black families met on Sunday mornings and evenings. The proximity of the church to the ball field made the Blake property the nexus of our small world.

The church events that I looked forward to most were the "deep water" baptisms held three or four times a year. The creek was not deep enough for total immersion of new Christian converts, so a large hole was dug, complete with steps leading into the five-foot baptizing pool that was lined with concrete. Because there was no way to get enough water to fill it up without a bucket brigade from the Blake well, the local volunteer fire department agreed to fill up the pool with their tanker truck. Arrival of the fire truck the Saturday before a Sunday baptizing ceremony was an auspicious event. The white volunteer firemen seemed to treat with great respect their role in filling up the small but deep pool and demonstrated almost ceremonial solemnity during their task. They seemed to know that the water they were pumping out of their truck would soon be sanctified as holy. After the pool was filled, it was carefully covered with a plastic canopy until the next day.

On Sunday, the adult baptismal candidates would emerge from dressing areas in the Blake house wrapped in white sheets. After impassioned prayers and singing, the initiate would be dunked backward into the water as the preacher, who was also partially submerged in the water, tightly held the initiate's nose. On several occasions, I observed the ceremony from high in a tree by the woods, like Nicodemus in the Bible craning his neck to see Jesus, as the emergence of the newly baptized Christians from the water caused a wave of emotion that would pass through the encircling congregation. The new Christian would often swoon and fall into the arms of women attendants draped in white, who were fully prepared to deal with high levels of religious ecstasy. The newly baptized Christians knew that just as they had once emerged from their mother's womb in their physical birth, they were now "twice-born," or born again into the spiritual world of Jesus Christ, and were saved from death for all eternity, their sins now washed away by the blood of Jesus.

This simple form of Christianity made a deep impression on me. In contrast, I was raised in the rigidly doctrinal German Lutheran Church, with its strict formalities and elaborate rituals. I found the Blakes and the citizens of Georgetown to be uniformly nonjudgmental, caring, tolerant, and forgiving of the prejudice that surrounded them and affected almost every aspect of their lives.

A tight bond of fellowship ran through the congregation, which seemed bound together by this simple church with its wood stove, secondhand pews, tar paper walls, tambourines, and bass drum. The church formed a community and offered a message of hope to these poor people. I imagined that I was observing how the religion of Jesus had formed two thousand years before, growing out of small, simple house gatherings of hopeful believers. Like the inhabitants of Georgetown, most of the early Christians were members of the oppressed underclass of the day, whose hope lay in a world far beyond this one. The message focused on the "Good News," the idea that Jesus offered the promise for justice in the next world and eternal life for all Christians. This hope must have made the poverty and racism in this part of the world easier to bear.

What then could be going on in the church those frigid Sundays, long after the last parishioner had departed for home down the dirt path that ran through Georgetown? When the coast was clear, about two o'clock in the afternoon, Fox or his brother Sam would direct across the woods toward our farm a finely tuned Tarzan yell, the sound of which would resonate in the small valley between our houses. The Blake brothers knew my Sunday routine. I would come home from church, eat my mother's traditional Sunday dinner of fried chicken, creamed corn, rice and gravy, green peas, home-made biscuits, and heavily sweetened iced tea with lemon. When I responded with my own version of a Tarzan yell, it meant that I was coming soon and that they were to hold the card game until I arrived.

I would hurdle the fence that held in our family's assortment of farm animals, many raised just for the pleasure they brought. This might consist of ten to twenty cows and their calves, a bull for breeding, several hogs and piglets, chickens, a duck or two, several sheep, including my pet sheep, Cotton, whom I had raised from a lamb with baby bottles of warmed milk after her mother had died, my donkey Jack and his mother, sometimes a few goats, and our horses Star and Prancer.

Once I cleared the fence, dodging farm animals and sidestepping their readily identifiable piles of manure in the pasture, and reached the woods, I was free and clear from the sight of my parents. I usually told them I was going to "play over at the Blakes" for the afternoon. I left my older sister to read, my father to take his Sunday afternoon nap, and my mother to clean up the kitchen after the masterful feast she had prepared. It was important to get away before any Sunday afternoon visitors arrived.

Through the woods, over the creek, up the hill, across the scrub pasture I would sprint, then carefully sneak to the back of the church. Entering through the back door, I would look to see who had gathered for the afternoon. I was usually the fourth person to join the clandestine activity planned for that afternoon: a card game we called "bid whiz."

Bid whiz, formally known as bid whist, was a fast form of bridge. Cards would be dealt to the four players, and bids would be made by each player according to how many "tricks" each predicted he and his partner could take by playing the highest card in a round. The person opposite you at the table automatically became your partner in the game. The player who predicted taking the most hands chose the trump card and would lead off the game by casting the first card.

The real art of the game was for a player to figure out the strengths and weaknesses of his partner's hand and calculate how the two hands could complement each other without wasting valuable trump cards on tricks that could be taken with a high, non-trump card. If one met one's predicted bid of tricks, so many points were assigned toward a total score. Bonus points were allotted for each trick exceeding a bid, but a heavy penalty was applied if you fell short. The penalty increased with the size of the shortfall.

Our games took on a life of their own with joking, taunting, and yells of exultation at a masterfully executed trump, such as the appearance of an ace after the opponent felt certain that all the trumps had been played out. Hence, as in regular bridge, everything depended first on the ability to keep track of which cards had been played and second, on the secret codes used with one's partner to communicate the valuable cards each held.

Games could go on for hours and hours with debits and credits added or subtracted from the number of points required for winning. The game was occasionally interrupted for someone to restock the wood stove or for someone to relieve himself, usually out the back door on the pasture side between the hog pen and the church. The hogs in the pen behind the church gave little notice. Too much traffic from the church to the family outhouse might be observed by Miss Ruth and arouse her suspicion that "somethin's goin' on out there in the church."

When victory came for a winning team, there were cries of pride and exultation and appropriately insulting remarks were made to the losing pair, who inevitably argued about who was responsible for any mistakes made in the strategy that led to the defeat. Boyce's older brother Johnny, in particular, was unbearable in victory. When Johnny won, you could count on hearing about his victory in detail for weeks. Only a crushing and decisive win against Johnny would shut him up. Even then, such a victory would buy his silence for only a short while until he would win again, and then the cycle would begin all over. There were few pleasures I relished more as a boy than to beat Johnny Blake at bid whiz.

Miss Ruth had issued a clear edict against playing ball and cards on Sunday. To be caught playing cards in the church was unthinkably sacrilegious, but we took careful measures to keep from being discovered. One of us would be positioned for a clear view of the Blake house in case Miss Ruth was to notice smoke coming out of the church chimney and appear unexpectedly. She was a formidable presence, but if we saw her heading in the direction of the church, the cards could be put away quickly. Whenever she did come into the church, there would be no evidence of our illicit activity. Our small and obviously guilty congregation would claim that we were "just talkin'." Miss Ruth would shake her head suspiciously but rarely bothered to ask more questions. She knew our crafty group was unlikely to be caught at whatever we were doing. Besides,

Sunday was Miss Ruth's day to rest a bit and was not to be spent playing detective in uncovering our secret card games.

There was one thing, however, that could not only interrupt a game but destroy a whole afternoon just when your team might be on the verge of triumph—and that was a surprise visit by Donna. Donna was Boyce's youngest sister, nicknamed "Pumpkin" but called "Punkin." On the surface, Punkin appeared to be a darling, engaging little girl, unquestionably the family pet. Evidently, the name Punkin was applied to her because of her almost perfectly round face and deep-set dark eyes that seemed to twinkle and shine from within, conveying an infinitely happy nature. Punkin was perpetually spoiled with candy and Moon Pies, which were her favorite, because no one could bear to say no to her.

On the other hand, there was a diabolical side to Punkin's personality. She was easily bribed by her older sisters with candy to try to catch us playing cards. Punkin's small stature enabled her to stealthily negotiate unnoticed through the Blake yard between the church and house. She would hide behind piles of split wood, small shrubs, and the giant, black cast-iron boiling pots. Punkin might suddenly appear like a small, dark apparition at the church window before she was detected and, in a flash, head back toward the house to her mother, all the while chanting: "Muh! Boyce, Sam, Tom, Johnny, and Zeke are playing cards in the church! Muh! Muh! Boyce, Sam, Tom, and Zeke . . ."

Punkin's betrayal inevitably meant the imminent appearance of Miss Ruth, usually with broom in hand, at the door of the Blakes' house. She would call out, "You boys get out of that church right now! How many times do I have to tell you to stay out of that church unless it's to talk to the Lord? This time I'm really goin' to tear up some hide!"

Caught guilty in the act by Punkin, the card players would scramble out the back door of the church, as we feared that things would be much worse if Miss Ruth actually charged across the yard with that broom to chase us out, much as Jesus had once chased the money changers out of the Temple in Jerusalem. We knew that Miss Ruth would cool down in time, that we could claim innocence since she hadn't actually seen us in action, or that Punkin might be counter-bribed with Moon Pies to retract her accusation, but for the time being, Punkin would have successfully dismantled our game. There was also the matter as to which Blake sister had set her up to turn us in to Miss Ruth. Punkin never acted alone. Miss Ruth sometimes sent her on the mission, but generally she was sent by a sister in retaliation toward one of the brothers for some offense committed during the course of the week, or even longer ago. The Blake sisters had long memories.

If the game had been interrupted at a particularly critical stage, for instance, at a point when one team was on the brink of victory, and if the weather wasn't that bad, we would resume the game deep in the woods. There was some advantage to the Blake brothers in delaying their return home, as the extra time allowed Miss Ruth to "get over it," or allowed for the possibility that somebody might arrive early for a visit before Sunday night church and thus provide a welcome distraction. Too, she would not continue her barrage in front of Sunday afternoon guests. Experience reassured the Blake brothers that after church, all would be forgiven anyway.

In retrospect, I suspect that Miss Ruth, along with her husband, Johnson, knew exactly where their boys were and what we all were doing. The shows of broom-shaking outrage precipitated by Punkin's most recent report on our behavior were perfunctory shows of disapproval on the part of Miss Ruth. I imagine now that both of the Blake parents must have enjoyed watching our panicked exodus from the church's back door and rear windows as Miss Ruth tried to "scare us good." They likely figured it was better for us to be in church doing whatever we might be doing rather than anywhere else outside of their purview.

The parents' collective wisdom was correct because we would never think to drink alcohol or smoke even rabbit tobacco in the church. Some things really were sacred, and what we were sharing in the church was a friendship that would last a lifetime. God would not disapprove of that.

Our times growing up were focused on boyish things of the moment, like competing to see who could cleanly split wood the fastest for either the Blake or the Stoudemire fire, catching one of my fugitive piglets on the loose, building a dam at the creek, outdoing each other with an overhand hoop shot and developing new finesse in a lay-up move.

Eventually, I would have to leave this little farm and the woods and the pasture ball field where we would play till dark when the ball was barely visible. I'd leave the Blakes' little Holiness Church, where we had played bid whiz for hours as if lost in a dream. Once gone, I knew that water still ran through our creek, but I knew, too, that there were no more children happily digging up clay and mud to fill in the makeshift dams we would construct with rocks and old boards in an effort to create a place we hoped might be large enough and deep enough for swimming.

The next torrential rain always washed away our dams and our big dreams. We never figured out how to build in overflow pipes that would keep the water from washing over and dissolving our dams. But we never stopped trying. When one dam was washed away, we would do a careful analysis, then try again with bigger rocks, stronger boards, more mud. We eventually tried to add clay pipes at the top so the water would flow through them and not over the dam itself when a big rain came. We figured that once we finally made a dam that would hold firm, we would catch some fish from a nearby farmer's pond, stock the swimming hole, and do some real fishing in our very own small pond. We had grand schemes.

We never did quite get it right. Another rain would inevitably come and wash away all our hard work. The hard rains, however, never washed away our hope of building the ideal swimming hole and fishing pond. Even now as an adult, I sometimes turn over in my mind ways we might have built the dams so they would have lasted. I still can't figure out what we might have done differently.

West of Eden

Life and Work in the Garden

> We shall not cease from exploration,
> And the end of all our exploring
> Will be to arrive where we started
> And know the place for the first time.

> —T. S. Eliot, "Little Gidding"

A short distance across the woods on our farm, work was not just a necessity—it amounted to a sacred and holy ritual. My father had instilled in me a strong Puritan work ethic, a Depression-era fear of, and need to be prepared at all times for, economic catastrophe, from which you could protect yourself only by working unrelentingly and saving every penny, nickel, dime, piece of twine, bent nail, and broken board, anything that had a remote possibility of being useful in the future. Work was the thing, and the only thing.

This almost complete dedication to work served him well in his position as the much-respected head agricultural agent for Lincoln County. Most of the farmers in the county worked as hard and as long as my father did. Farming dominated the life of the outlying county, and the title of county agent carried great prestige within the farming community. My father's office was located in the county courthouse. His primary job was to provide expert advice to the local farmers on how to grow crops and take care of their farm animals. With the help of several assistant agents, he ran this state-funded program, which was a branch of the state's agricultural college and formally called the Agricultural Extension Service.

The county agent was known by almost everyone in the county, from the housewife who needed advice on what sort of pesticide to use to protect her roses from infamous Japanese beetles to the dairy farmer who would call "Mr. George" in the middle of the night because his cow was "swollen and down with the bloat." The county agent was part agricultural scientist, part fertilizer and seed consultant, and often amateur veterinarian. Without question, he was the local herbicide and pesticide expert. My father provided guidance on what crops to grow on what type of land so as to offer the best yields; how to rotate the planting of crops from year to year so as not to deplete the soil's natural nutrients; what herbicides to use to kill fungi and the appropriate amounts to apply.

Another branch of his office was the Home Extension Service, whose female agents under my father's supervision provided classes and advice for the women of the county on practical matters that supported farm life, including cooking; making various jellies and preserves; canning vegetables in glass quart jars; freezing meats; making sausage; sewing; and setting a family budget, which was always a precarious task complicated by the inevitable fluctuation of farm income from year to year. These agents organized and led Home Demonstration Clubs, where these techniques were taught, discussed, and practiced. Raising flowers was an active component of the Home Demonstration Clubs. At least once a year, a county show would be held by the clubs from the various small communities with displays of cakes, pies, canned vegetables, and embroidered homemade quilts.

Among the farm youth, my father was known as the organizer and supervisor of 4-H clubs, which was the heart of this rural community—a club for farmers' kids with an official name that stood for Home, Heart, Health, and Happiness. These rural youth groups, with their pragmatic emphasis on skills related to farming, were far more active in the county than the well-scrubbed, church-based, knot-tying Boy Scouts in town. These were just a few of the responsibilities that fell under my father's area of expertise and responsibility, and he relished every minute of his work.

There was no such thing as a telephone answering service for reaching my father. His name was in the telephone book, and he got calls at all hours of the day and night. The dairy farmers rose the earliest. Their calls would begin at home as early as four o'clock in the morning. The oddest call I remember Mr. George receiving came around sunrise one morning from a newly widowed farm wife who wanted to know what she should do about a dead rooster in the road in front of her house. The rooster had escaped his pen and was killed by a hit-and-run driver. The elderly lady wanted to know how she could get someone in the county to remove the rooster. I remember hearing my father patiently say, "Don't worry, I'll take care of it." Although he never mentioned the call to the family, I assume that he drove out to her farm and removed the deceased rooster himself. My father was always completely accommodating, regardless of the circumstances. Not once did I ever hear him speak in a rude or condescending way to his early-morning or late-night callers. He had the greatest respect for the farmer. He knew that their lives were financially unpredictable, and that most of them lived from hand to mouth from year to year, based on the eternally fluctuating nature of the weather. Some of the farmers had little education and could not read. Thinking back to the times when I would tag along with him on his field visits to these farmers, I realize my father was a master at translating complex principles of agricultural science into language that was understandable to these men, as well as a master at making the information practical and useful for them.

One of his stranger veterinary duties was to teach chicken farmers how to "de-beak" their chickens. Debeaking a chicken meant the slightly gruesome task of cutting off part of their upper beak with a red-hot cauterizing steel clamp that resembled a small, miniature guillotine. In spite of the crude nature of the procedure, it was painful primarily to the person such as myself who had been conscripted into the job of catching and holding the chickens by their struggling legs as they attempted to peck their way free while this minor chicken-house surgery was performed. The procedure occurred in barns where hens were kept by the hundreds and even thousands. Debeaking was considered an agricultural necessity so that chickens would not peck each other to death in their overcrowded housing arrangements and to keep them from breaking each other's eggs.

Dehorning cattle was important because horns can grow so large and sharp that they pose a danger to other cows and to the farmer. This was accomplished by the use of large steel pincers that would amputate the horns. The process of dehorning young calves required the use of electrically heated branding irons applied to the roots of their pubescent horns. By thus cauterizing the nascent horn, future growth would be prevented. Dehorning older cows and bulls with full-grown horns was a much more complex and dangerous endeavor.

First, the surgical patient had to be roped, sometimes from a horse, then led and pushed into a barn, where they were securely tied to a post. Next, a large steel pincer was slipped around the base of the horn and clamped shut near the skin of the animal's skull. It was my impression that this procedure was painless enough to the animal and that the tight rope about their neck hurt more than cutting off the relatively nerveless horn. The swift procedure could be gruesome, however, since the lower part of the horn next to the cowhide had blood vessels that would sometimes spurt in pulses for a time until my father controlled the bleeding by compression and by application of a mysterious white powder he called "alum." I still have not identified this magic substance that almost immediately stopped the oozing of blood from the gaping hole at the base of the hapless animal's skull.

I would collect the larger horns, allow them to dry out over a period of weeks until the interior cartilaginous substance of the horn dried out, shrank, and fell away, at which time the inside of the horn could be scraped clean with rough sandpaper. With a little further cleaning, the horn could be used to drink from, as I imagined the Vikings used to do. The outside of the horn could be smoothed down with the very finest sandpaper and then polished with wax. In the frontier days, the wide end of the horn was capped with a piece of stretched leather and tied on snugly. Then a small hole was cut at the pointed end of the horn and plugged so that it could be used to store and dispense gunpowder for the muskets and long rifles of the early settlers.

Another medical procedure performed in the barnyard involved young male pigs that were castrated so that their meat would be more tender when they were slaughtered as full-grown hogs. My father accomplished the castrations with his razor-sharp knife that was sterilized with a match and alcohol, followed by an antiseptic spray. Castrating young bulls for the same purpose meant using a huge iron clamp that was placed around the base of their testicles. The clamp was brought firmly together by squeezing the wooden handles of the instrument for an excruciating few minutes as the young bull struggled against the rope that tied him firmly to a post or tree. Doctor Freud would have shuddered to see these farm operations. He could have written several books on the effects these crude veterinary procedures might have had on the psyches of young farm boys such as myself conscripted to assist in them. I admit that I spent a number of hours discussing that subject from my psychoanalyst's couch in later years during my training. It did not take much imagination to inspire fear that the same procedures could possibly be applied to my own anatomy.

Through performing and teaching these and other techniques, my father came to know every farmer in Lincoln County. He spent about half of his time in the field, making calls on farmers who might need him to take a look at a suspicious fungus on their crop of beans, a strange insect that needed to be eradicated from a field of corn, a cow with red and swollen udders who would not let her calf feed, or a rowdy and unreasonable bull who defied any efforts at being "dehorned." These were just a few of the nearly endless small and large problems he was called upon day and night to address.

I often accompanied my father on these calls to the farmers, and I was very proud to be known as "Little George," so called because farmers instantly recognized our family resemblance. By riding with my father on these visits, I learned not only about every farmer and his family, but also every back road in the county. I grew to feel as great a respect for these people and the difficult lives they led as my father felt.

Life for the small southern farmer was dangerous at times. I knew more than one farmer who had been crushed by an overturned tractor, and one family in which a father and son had been overcome by gases in the depths of a deep grain silo. When the son saw his father collapse in the interior of the silo, overcome by the methane gases, the son went to rescue him and suffered the same fate. I remember attending their double funeral. Occasionally, a farmer would be killed by his own rifle or shotgun when he was "crossing a fence" while hunting. When such hunting accidents occurred while the farmer was alone, it generally meant the farmer had gone

BOYCE BLAKE (1951-1997)

PAUL "SKIP" LAWING (1950-1972)
KILLED IN ACTION, VIETNAM

JEB SEAGLE (1953-1983)
KILLED IN ACTION, GRENADA

NORTH STATE HOTEL (1848/52-1968)

DANIEL A KANIPE (1853-1926)
SEVENTH U.S. CAVALRY

ROBERT JOHNSTON (1837-1919)
CONFEDERATE GENERAL

PLEASANT RETREAT ACADEMY (1817)

CITY LUNCH (ESTABLISHED AT THIS LOCATION IN 1921)

ROBERT F. HOKE (1837-1912)
CONFEDERATE GENERAL

STEPHEN D. RAMSEUR (1837-1864)
CONFEDERATE GENERAL

VFW Clubhouse (1958)

Lithia Springs Inn (late 1850s-1940)

JERRY CRUMP (1933-1977)
MEDAL OF HONOR, KOREA

DR. BOYCE GRIGGS (1919-1992)

OSCAR SLOAN STEWART
(1868-1954)

ASMAN MCBRYDE STOUDEMIRE
(1881-1959)

GEORGE AND LOUISE STOUDEMIRE   SYLVIA WITH GEORGE STOUDEMIRE

GEORGE AND LOUISE STOUDEMIRE WITH STEWART, ALAN, AND SYLVIA

LOUISE STOUDEMIRE WITH
ALAN AND SYLVIA

STEWART STOUDEMIRE

ALAN STOUDEMIRE

ALAN STOUDEMIRE

to the woods and committed suicide, because everyone knew to unload guns before crossing a difficult or high fence, and moreover, it was hard to imagine shooting oneself in the process. These are only a few examples of the family farm tragedies that I recall.

America still nourishes the myth of the simple, noble, and happy life of the farmer. Most of the farmers in Lincoln County lived on relatively small plots of land and barely made a living of it. A farmer who owned more than one hundred acres was considered "land rich," but more times than not was "cash poor." Whether they had large or small farms, they rarely held insurance of any sort. If they could not work due to illness or injury, one of their cash crops might fail unless relatives or neighbors helped them out. If the farm carried a mortgage, a series of bad weather seasons could lead to foreclosure on the land by the lender, and that meant economic ruin. The life of the small southern farmer was arduous and accompanied by quiet, yet unremitting, year-to-year anxieties.

Still, farming in Lincoln County was a highly valued and time-honored profession that was often a family tradition dating back sometimes to Revolutionary days. Land was traditionally passed down in families from one generation to the next and was rarely sold to anyone outside a tight circle of relatives.

The farms of the county had sweeping fields of oats, wheat, barley, corn, and soybeans. By the 1950s, there were a few cotton fields remaining, but cotton had become unprofitable as a cash crop and was fading from the farm scene in that part of the world. In the far western parts of the county in the coolness of higher elevations closer to the mountains, apple trees grew well. Eventually, large apple orchards would be planted there, primarily due to my father's encouragement and enthusiasm for the idea. He foresaw the potential in the crop as a source of predictable income for the farmers, given the hardiness of apple trees. He ultimately convinced the famous National Fruit Products Company with their White House label to build a small processing plant for making apple juice and sauce on the site of one of the larger orchards, so that it was possible to put apples into production within hours of being plucked from their trees.

Dairy farms also covered the land with relatively small, but proud herds of Guernsey, Jersey, and Holstein milk cows. Only a few farmers raised beef cattle such as black Angus and Herefords, owing to the fact that fattening the animals for slaughter required large tracts of cleared pasture land. Lincoln County was originally a forest. The fields that now existed had been carved out of the landscape with great effort. Farmers had to constantly beat back the unceasing attempts by the wilderness to reclaim its lost land.

The land surrounding Lincolnton ranged from the steep foothills of the Blue Ridge Mountains in the west to the rolling forested hills and pasturelands toward the east. It was lush land, frequently crisscrossed by small streams that merged into tributaries of the Catawba River that flowed through adjacent Mecklenburg County to the east. The South Fork of the Catawba River cut through the middle of the county, where the town of Lincolnton was centrally located.

Little farm settlements were situated throughout the county at crossings of small roads near country stores and churches. The farmers would gather at these crossings on Saturdays and Sundays to talk about the weather, politics, and religion. The small rural communities had curious names like Cat Square, so called because people were said to bring their unwanted litters of cats there to leave in hopes of their adoption. Many of the cats stayed around to wander about homeless, but they were generally well fed from scraps that the farmers and their families would toss to the abandoned creatures who grew wild over time.

There were the communities known as Hog Hill, named for obvious reasons, and Pumpkin Center, so named as my father told me, because pumpkins seemed to grow so well in this part of the county. Other communities included Buffalo Shoals, where buffalo were said to roam along the river in days when the Cherokees claimed the land; Reepsville, the home of the Reep clan, descendants of the local Revolutionary War hero Adam Reep; Iron Station, Miss Ruth's original home, with its rich iron ore deposits and the site of once-great, fiery smelting furnaces like the Vesuvius; Vale, derived from Valhalla, the German home of the Teutonic gods and like its mythical namesake, a place of great peace and beauty; Bear Ridge, where a harmless black bear who had wandered down from the mountains had been caught and kept in a pen at a country store in order to attract curious farm families who would gather to gawk at the pathetic creature. A variety of communities were named for the nearest water supply or branch of the river, such as North Brook, Howard's Creek, and Indian Creek. I loved these little settlements with their simple farms and solid, earnest, hardworking people, who had over the past several hundred years held fast to their land, as well as their heritage, identity, and individualism.

With the exception of the small family farms that were scattered about the county, the landscape had changed little from what the first Scots-Irish and German settlers beheld over 250 years ago. It was easy for me to imagine how the first European peasant farmers must have gaped in initial disbelief, then become entranced and fallen in love with the land that lay before them. This land offered not only undreamed of prosperity to people who had once owned almost nothing they could call their own in Europe, but also complete freedom to live as they saw fit.

Many if not most of the families who settled the county had easily identifiable descendants still living in

Lincoln County today. As I gradually delved into the history of the county, I was amazed to recognize so many of the names of its earliest pioneers. They were the very same names of my friends from school, from church, the same names of my parents' friends, the same names of the farmers with whom my father worked. The German family names were the most distinctive: Reinhardt, Heavner, Huss (Hauss), Cline (Klein), Costner, Warlick, Baumgardner, Lineberger, Froneberger, Ramseur, Mullen, Rudisill, Seagle, Yoder, Schenck, Rhyne, Forney, Mauney, Kaiser, and so forth. Few of Lincoln's settlers ever seemed to leave the county, especially those whose families owned farmland, and it seemed that those who did leave would eventually return.

Our farm and the neighboring rural black community of Georgetown lay near the center of the county seat of Lincolnton ("Lincoln Town") and only about three miles from town by way of paths through the woods. Nevertheless, in such a little place as Lincolnton, being a few miles from the center of town would easily qualify for living "in the country." The surrounding county merged gently and almost unnoticeably with the outskirts of town. When I was a boy, Lincolnton's population was no more than five thousand, with several thousand more thinly distributed in the county.

At the center of town on a beautiful square of lush, green lawn amidst huge ancient oak trees stood the stately and impressive Greek-revival granite courthouse with huge columns that would have rivaled those of the Parthenon. The courthouse contained various offices for county affairs, including that of my father. From his window, my father could view the town's most prominent historical marker on the courthouse lawn, a memorial to the Lincoln County Confederate veterans. It was erected by the Daughters of the Confederacy, most of whom could claim to be direct descendants of these young Lincoln County Confederates.

A road encircled the courthouse square, and other roads, including Main Street, extended outward from the square like spokes of a wheel. The word *town*, when used to refer to Lincolnton, bordered on being a misnomer. With the granite courthouse where my father's office was stationed as its hub, most of the town consisted of a handful of small shops and churches that could be found on the principal thoroughfare of East Main Street. East Main Street extended eastward from the courthouse square with a half-mile stretch of small establishments: two drugstores; two barber shops; post office; two dimestores; the clothing store of Mr. Dave Lerner, whose family was the only Jewish one I knew of in Lincolnton and for whom I worked on Saturdays after I turned sixteen; several ladies' dress shops; one movie theater replete with a balcony where blacks were required to sit; and two grandiloquent Baptist and Methodist churches.

Small, heavily shaded, all-white neighborhoods surrounded and spread out from the courthouse–Main Street nexus with two large furniture factories on the far fringes of town. The furniture factories were owned by the fathers of two of my grade-school girlfriends, each of whom at one time or another had been the object of my unrequited love, Carole Cochrane and Becky Burris. It was not that they were the richest girls in town, but in my eyes, the most beautiful and desirable. It seemed that their combination of both wealth and beauty also made them unobtainable, which they always remained to me.

The "black" part of town, called "Freedom," was located on the edge of the town limits. Its original name was "Freedman," denoting the community's origins in the days of Reconstruction when the area was populated by former slaves. The city's once all-white cemetery served as an approximate dividing area between the all-white and all-black sections of town. The African Methodist Episcopal Zion church that Boyce's great-uncle Reverend Hilliard Blake once pastored was located in Freedom, still stands there, and is now well over one hundred years old.

Within only a few mile's radius, the township began to merge with small farms that grew larger the farther one drove out along one of the four main roads that served as the links to the wider world. Within a few miles, one was decidedly "in the country," where Georgetown and our farm were located.

My father George was the complete and unquestioned master of our own farm operation, which took on the characteristics of an agricultural experimentation station. George felt he could not advise farmers expertly unless "I've done it or grown it myself." Hence, every variety of animal was born on this Noah-like farm. Some of the animals, like my donkey Jack and my sheep Cotton, served the family cause in other ways. These two characters were loaded up each Christmas to star in our Lutheran Church's live Nativity scene.

The barnyard was fully "integrated," except for the pigs, who required a special meshed fence because they were master escape artists, particularly if they sniffed a tasty root beyond the confines of the fence. They would follow the scent with their muddy snouts to temporary freedom. If they got this far, the fugitives would head straight to the family garden for a feast of sweet potatoes, their delicacy of choice.

One year, like a cloud of locusts, a herd of piglets descended upon my entire ninety-foot row of sweet potatoes—leaf, vine, root, and potato—planted and meticulously tended as part of a 4-H demonstration project. By the time I discovered their crime, the guilty porcine parties were nowhere to be seen. I finally found them in the hay of the barn sleeping piled upon each other and mute about any role in the decimation of my prized patch of potatoes. They could barely be aroused from their sweet potato slumber to be herded back to their concerned and aggravated mother.

It was difficult when a favorite cow or pig ended up on our kitchen table, on which occasion some member of my family would announce that a former farm pet with a name like "Elsie" or "Betsy" was being eaten that night. Such a morbid pronouncement led to a mood of gloom and guilt that hovered over the meal.

The three pigs who had become my pets seemed to be the hardest to eat. I had given them the biblical names of Shadrach, Meshach, and Abednego after the three faithful Hebrews who had survived the fiery furnaces of some nefarious Babylonian king—Nebuchadnezzar, I believe. My three pigs, however, were not able to escape the heat of Louise Stoudemire's oven. Shadrach, Meshach, and Abednego ended up as bacon, pork roast, sausage, and pork chops over a period of time that seemed endless to me.

We eventually quit naming our animals, unless they were prize cows for the 4-H shows, which guaranteed the animals' perpetual reprieve from slaughter or sale. A retired show cow could look forward to a comfortable retirement on our farm until it died a natural death, at which time it was rewarded with a grave in the woods and a modest rock marker with its name carved on it.

My pampered and thoroughly spoiled dairy calf, Missy, was treated like the other show cows, brushed every day, her tail hair carefully combed and braided, her hooves manicured and polished. Every effort was made to pet them so they would behave at the annual county 4-H show, where they were paraded about a circus-like ring surrounded by proud farmer parents.

We would spend the night before the annual 4-H Show sleeping in the hay with our cows in the barn on the show grounds to make sure that the prized contestants didn't get dirty by carelessly lying down to sleep in their own manure. We wanted to be sure, too, that they slept well on a full stomach so that they would not be unduly nervous or rowdy the next day at the big event. Ribbons were handed out by the judges in rank order of blue, red, or white, based on grooming, showmanship, and a variety of physical characteristics such as the shapeliness of the cow's physical contours, including the width and proportions of their posteriors and the shapeliness and fullness of their udders. The annual 4-H show was a bovine beauty pageant taken no less seriously by us than the Miss America Pageant in Atlantic City. The more I think of it, the two events were more alike than they were different. Unruly and embarrassing behavior by one's cow at this important annual event decreased the animal's chances of being shown again in the future and, likewise, decreased the probability of its being allowed to reach a ripe old age on the farm as reward for its service in these agricultural beauty pageants.

In addition to the attention given to the animals, the fruits and vegetables grown by my father were zealously tended to as well. Every variety that could be grown at our latitude was planted, including corn, string beans, lima beans, turnips and their greens, carrots, kale, onions, radishes, beets, cabbage, okra, strawberries, blueberries, cucumbers, Irish potatoes, sweet potatoes, pumpkin (not be confused with the pesky Punkin Blake), watermelons, squash, green peas, black-eyed peas, gourds, and many species of tomatoes. Acres of large grain crops would be planted, too. The grain from these crops would be stored as feed for the cows and hogs. The hay had to be bailed in the fall of the year, loaded onto trailers, unloaded, and stored in the barn so as to provide feed for the cows and horses in the winter.

Not all of these crops could be found on the Stoudemire farm at any given time because my father, George, was always in an experimenting mode of thinking and would scientifically rotate his crops from year to year, always trying out something new. He wanted to see which pesticide or herbicide would work best on which crops, so he could talk about his own personal experiences with the farmers in a knowledgeable way.

The cows on the farm would be fed twice a day in the barn. George trained them well. When we hollered, "whooo-up! whooo-up!" across the pasture and woods, the amiable beasts would come at an ambling trot in a slow race to see who would get to the barn first and thus claim the best position at the trough for the day's hay and feed. While the mothers chowed down on the hay, the young calves would take the opportunity of their mother's contentment to eat dinner, as well, by gently nudging and suckling at their udders. The well-fed, satisfied families then retired for the evening to the pasture for a chew of cud, while the young calves played with each other, usually by butting heads. The young bulls, of course, were the most masterful at the sport of butting heads, while the more demure young heifers politely refrained from such activity if the young bulls became too rough or obnoxious with each other. The older cows and bulls would meander around appearing bored by their offspring's after-dinner antics, unless a mother cow saw her young calf getting the worse of it from some young, rambunctious bull. In this case, mom would intervene by butting him gently, yet decisively, away.

George's pride and joy were his muscadine grapes. Even Fox and I knew that muscadines were good for only three limited human purposes: making unbearably sweet homemade wine that usually turned out so bad no one could drink enough even to get drunk on; snacking on the grapes in quantities sufficiently small enough to avoid getting the bellyache; and finally, making jelly, its best use. In spite of what we considered their relative uselessness given the amount of work it took to maintain them, the vineyard was prized by George.

My father set up several beehives beside the vineyard because he believed the bees not only supplied us with incredibly delicious, warm honey straight off the honeycomb, but the industrious insects also facilitated pollination in the vineyard and among the various plants and flowers about the farm, thus increasing their productivity. The bees became familiar with our human smell and were gentle creatures unless you tried to raid their honey, a task my father always assumed. I can remember sitting quietly within several feet of their hives, while I watched them come and go and perform little dances for each other. My father explained that the dances were a way for them to communicate directions to rich sources of flower pollen. There were thousands of bees in these hives, and I cannot remember ever being stung by even one of them.

When our tractor broke down every now and then, we borrowed a plowing mule named Cake from our neighbor, Mr. Armstrong. I remember the codes for the mule that my father would call out: "Gee" was turn right, "Haw" was turn left, and of course, "Giddy-up" was go, and "Whoa!" was stop. I remember, too, my father putting me to bed as a child with his stories about "Alan the Mule" and his many adventures. Alan was a fun-loving, adventurous young mule who was always getting himself into various predicaments. In these stories, Alan the Mule would generally extricate himself from his predicaments, find his way home, and like the mule version of James Bond, always manage to come out on top.

I suspect my father was telling these stories to help me gain an understanding of something about myself and my stubborn, mule-like nature. He was right in most respects about the similarities between my personality and that of Alan the Mule. When he became frustrated with a farmer who was not following his advice, he would say that trying to get "So-and-So" to do something was like "trying to get a mule to climb a ladder." He likely thought of me in the same way when I was stubborn about some farm task he expected me to do. In spite of my mule-like characteristics, I usually went up whatever "ladder" my father ordered me to climb.

In later years, my father displayed a gentler side to his agricultural interests that surprised almost everyone. He became a dedicated rose gardener. He set about not just to raise roses, but to raise every variety that could be grown on American soil. In this pursuit, he displayed his characteristic zeal and obsessiveness. In time, he grew about four hundred rose bushes scattered over the property. The American Rose Society apparently had identified, classified, and certified 103 rose varieties known as *All American Roses*. My father decided to obtain and grow at least one variety of each of these types of roses, and he set about to do it. Over a period of ten years, he devoted himself with a passion to completing his collection, something he claimed that no one had ever been able to do in one location. Knowing this fact made him redouble his efforts. "Come hell or high water," he insisted, this epic rose garden was to be planted. Thus began the search across the country for cuttings of each variety of All American Rose.

When he had nearly completed his collection, he discovered there was one remaining very rare variety nicknamed Pinky, which he did not have. Apparently, it was an extremely difficult type of rose to raise on American soil. This challenge did not deter George. He advertised in several trade rose magazines, and one day, he received a call from an elderly man in a California nursing home who said he had been successful in growing Pinky. He further explained that he was willing for his wife to dig up and send my father not just a cutting of Pinky, but the entire plant: Pinky herself. Aware that his Pinky required special care, this gentleman was willing to give "her" to my father if my father promised to take "good care of her." They struck a deal, and before long, Pinky came by overnight delivery.

It was a proud day when my father finally believed he had completed his collection. For a number of years after Pinky's arrival at our farm, he received from the elderly gentleman a Christmas card in which he asked my father how Pinky was doing. My father dutifully responded, saying that Pinky was "doing fine," occupied a very special place in his rose garden, and received extra special attention, which was, of course, only Pinky's due, given her rarity and celebrity status among the collection.

I never knew whether my father ever really completed the collection, but he believed he had. Completing the collection was not nearly as important as the drive in him that the search inspired. My father undertook this task late in his life, and I think that just as the rose gradually unfolds and reveals its inner beauty in the long growing process, my father's final years disclosed a new part of George that finally, slowly unfolded. He revealed a softer and more gentle love of life, nature, and beauty that had been all but obscured by his tough work ethic and his strict disciplinarian, U.S. Army colonel demeanor. I believe that just as it was difficult for him to express that side of himself to others, it was almost impossible for him even to be consciously aware of it or to admit that it existed. I understand now that his tough exterior was necessary armor that had shielded him from the pain of the loss of his mother and from the deprivation and disappointments of the Depression years.

As a local newspaper article described him, my father was a "special breed of cat." He mixed and moved well with people from all walks of life and had a special genius for making complex agricultural ideas and techniques accessible to the most uneducated farmer. An intense student of human nature, he took a personal interest in each person he met. His manner was a mixture of gruff old bear, pussycat, and battle-experienced army colonel.

He would ask direct, often provocative, questions and give direct and equally provocative answers whenever he felt that someone was not being honest and direct with him, but he delivered his responses in a soft drawl that, when he was angry or irritated, could assume a razor-sharp edge. Years later, his obituary would describe him as "a man for all seasons and a friend for all times."

He was one of the most respected and beloved men of the county, and I was immensely proud when someone would recognize my name and remark, "Why, you must be George Stoudemire's boy!" Even many years after his death, as a middle-aged physician, I would occasionally meet an elderly farmer in a store or on the street who, upon seeing the resemblance between us, would stop me with a friendly hand extended and the greeting, "Why, you look just like your daddy!" Even as a grown man, I was proud to be recognized as such.

My father was a perfectionist in his work and in his moral life, and he expected the same sort of excellence in those who worked for him on our farm, at church, and on community projects. Serving on a variety of Lutheran church and Rotary Club committees, he assumed his various roles in the local community with pride. He was especially aware of his permanent position as the agricultural mayor of the county.

He possessed a remarkable ability to put people at ease with his joking manner. Showing no mercy to those he suspected of dishonesty or fakery, on the other hand, he could just as easily cut through hypocrisy with his quick mind and acid tongue. George would tolerate some degree of foolishness, but he had no tolerance for fools.

He believed in discipline, which he learned from serving as a lieutenant colonel in the United States Army. At the time, in the late 1930s, Clemson College was preparing young men to fight in what loomed ahead as the world's second global conflict. The stern military drills of the day were not the "play soldier" hazing that would come later to characterize so many southern tin-pot military academies, but deadly serious training when rumors of war had spread to the hills of South Carolina from a world away. Upperclassmen understood that they might have to put their training into practice overnight.

His Puritan work ethic was born of the Lutheran church, the Great Depression, his German ancestry, and the United States Army, where he served in the Armored "Cavalry" as a tank company commander. In later years, preferring to keep to himself what he had been through in the Pacific, he spoke little of the war. All he ever mentioned to me, which helped explain his silence, was that sometimes he could still smell human flesh burning. He expressed a particular dislike for war movies, because they made war look like a Hollywood game and not the horror he remembered. He avoided his Clemson class reunions, he said, because over half of his classmates had been killed in the war, and he found it depressing to go back to find so many of them missing. All of his three brothers served in and survived the war. My Uncle Bob was among the first wave of troops to liberate the extermination camp at Dachau, Germany. Like my father, Uncle Bob never spoke of what he witnessed there as the gates were opened by the young American soldiers.

My father was an avid reader of small agricultural journals, so that he could be up on everything for the farmers he needed to advise from day to day. He seemed to be invigorated by ideas of almost any sort and would readily attack some "absolute truth" on which the Lutheran minister or Sunday school teacher piously expounded. He was careful not to shake the faith of his fellow parishioners, but he wanted to make them think a bit about the theological soup they were spoon-fed that week. He seemed to enjoy taunting the preacher with intellectual questions about the Bible, such as the ponderous dilemma posed by this argument: "If Adam and Eve had only two male sons and one killed the other, then where did everybody else come from? And where exactly did Cain's wife come from following his banishment to the netherlands East of Eden? Unless there was a biblical character left out of the story somewhere," my father would continue, "then the good son Abel and his mother Eve might have some explaining to do." This was one type of irreverent prodding he delighted in, much to the chagrin of the preachers and the more pious Lutheran church ladies.

He had a knack for posing a problem in a Socratic way, planting a suggestion, and then arguing a blue streak in colorful and animated language if he thought he was right.

He would punctuate his conclusion with a distinctive dry wit. He was persuasive, but careful not to humiliate, and he always told me that "you can always learn from the other person's point of view, even if they're dead wrong."

What impressed most people about him was that in spite of his gruff, tough military demeanor, there was an unmistakable sense that he cared about and respected each person he met. He especially had empathy for the poor and disadvantaged, perhaps because he had grown up in difficult times and had experienced loss himself at the age of twelve when his mother died of cancer. He carried silent but special disdain for the rich, whom he viewed as generally greedy and preoccupied with getting or holding onto their money and their privilege. His most favorite phrase was, "To whom much is given, much is expected." He was a Democrat politically and socially.

My father's major weakness was his utter and complete devotion to work. Besides the mundane work required of me every morning and evening of the week, including feeding the cows and hogs, Saturday was the big workday on our farm. Saturdays required additional special work projects, like hoeing weeds out of endless rows of string beans, mowing the grape vineyard and the large lawn surrounding our house and barn, planting, harvesting, peeling, shucking, baling hay, or stringing and repairing razor-sharp barbed-wire fences.

Fox, Sam, or Tom would be hired by my father for the day to help us out. Before we were old enough to do the heavy work on the farm, my brother, Stewart, and Frank Blake had been his main workers on Saturdays. Now that Stewart was in college and Frank had moved away from Blake Hill in order to get a regular job, our crew was the next generation to inherit the Saturday tradition of work that continued without interruption until it was well past dark.

Other than digging postholes for fencing through the impossibly rocky ground of the farm, one of the most onerous duties was shoveling cow and horse manure out of the barn into a trailer that, when full, would then be distributed shovelful by shovelful onto the garden as "natural fertilizer." After a day of natural fertilizer duty, my mother would not allow me to enter the house until I was thoroughly soaped and hosed down in the yard. Only then could I enter to take an additional real bath. She would take charge of cleaning and salvaging the work clothes I had worn that day; sometimes they just had to be thrown away.

Shoveling manure was the only job that Fox and Sam refused to help me with, usually by extending some lame excuse as to why they couldn't work that day. For instance, they might say Miss Ruth or Johnson needed them. I knew the truth, but I could hardly blame them for abandoning me on those noxious days.

The day following a manure-shoveling assignment, the Blakes kept their distance from me until they were convinced I had been properly "deodorized." Johnny Blake took full advantage of the situation, as one might imagine, by taunting me with comments like, "SHOO WEE! It smells like ol' Zeke has been shoveling out the barn again for his daddy! Let's give this boy some extra room to air out!"

During a card game, he might stop suddenly, look around the room while dramatically sniffing the air about him, and ask, "What's that I smell? Sure smells like somebody's stepped in somethin' around here!" The Blake brothers would then make a great show of shifting their chairs away from me so as to avoid the smell Johnny claimed I was exuding while they snickered in amusement. These were some of Johnny's less obscene comments and jokes on the subject of my manure-shuffling duties. Manure jokes seemed to provide Johnny an endless source of amusement.

With the exception of shoveling manure, the Blake brothers and I worked side by side for hours on end every Saturday of the year. The only difference between us as workers was that Fox and Sam were paid a fair wage for their work. I was merely performing "my duty." My main source of income was selling the eggs I collected from the twenty or so laying hens we kept penned. I would set about cleaning and boxing the eggs in crates of a dozen each and sell them to our regular customers, who were neighbors in the area and a few families from our church.

The job we hated more than all others George assigned us was the picking up of rocks from pastures, fields, and gardens, a job generally left for the dead of winter when there was almost no "real work" to be done. It was not just that the task was physically difficult and boring, but, in our adolescent philosophical opinion, it was existentially meaningless and a complete waste of time. It was work created by my father purely for the sake of work.

Adjacent to the bricked porch at our back door was the red brick well house that covered the old hand-dug well, which was probably at least one hundred years old. The top of the well itself was covered with a concrete slab. The old well had gone dry when I was very young, and a new well had been drilled. The old one was of no use, except for the entertainment it provided Fox and me: several times, when my mother and father were away from home, I poured a gallon of gasoline down the dry hole and dropped a firecracker to the bottom in order to create a large, flaming explosion. During the days of the Cold War with Russia, I often imagined that, operating as a secret agent, I had lobbed a Molotov cocktail into a Communist hideout, flushing their agents out of hiding.

Although my father never became aware of my clandestine pyrotechnics, he had made up his mind that the old well was dangerous and had to be filled up with rocks. So rocks it was, now and forever more. Saturday after Saturday in the dead of winter, we would trudge through the fields as George drove his tractor and trailer. Following dutifully behind, we picked up rock after rock in unbearable monotony, and then unloaded them, hand to hand, to be transferred from the trailer and thrown down the well. Other than losing a game of bid whiz to Johnny Blake, the worst that could befall us was an edict from the colonel to pick up more rocks to fill up "that stupid well," as we commonly referred to the bottomless pit.

It was no small project. The well was at least five feet in diameter and a hundred feet deep, and most of the rocks we gathered could be held in one hand. It was a great day in our lives when George was satisfied that the well had been "capped" for all eternity and that all current and future generations of Lincoln County children were safe from falling down his well. Since I had become convinced the hole led straight to Hell, I felt a sense of relief myself.

Work was work. The general philosophy was that even when there was no really useful work to be done, one should work anyway. So we worked until there was no more daylight, but sometimes for good measure, George would insist on working by the lights of the tractor after dark. In my father's office, there hung a simple quote I assume was of biblical origin. He had it framed, and it read, "All things come to those who wait." My father had scribbled these words below it: "As long as you work like hell while you wait."

It was not that having fun or enjoying oneself was bad in itself, but in my father's belief system, every minute that one spent playing or doing something pleasurable could have been spent accomplishing something that would make the world a better place, make the place of someone else in the world better, or if nothing else, make the farm a better and less rocky place. If one was working to help other people, one was only doing his God-given duty. In addition, he believed that one must always be working to shore up those supplies in case the worst happened in whatever form "the worst" might arrive.

My mother was George's faithful partner in the business of running the farm. She was no less serious about the importance and value of being productive and staying busy. She, too, was a product of the Great Depression and possessed the morally strict, frugal, and independent heritage of her Scots-Irish ancestors. She understandably shared with my father a fearful dedication to an unrelenting work ethic that derived from the years of economic deprivation during the Depression and the hardships, uncertainties, and anxieties of the war years.

She was, nevertheless, a remarkably compassionate woman and, much like my father, could never say no to a soul in need. She was widely known for her generosity to the elderly and invalids, known in our community as "shut-ins," referring to the fact that these unfortunate souls had been shut in from the rest of the world due to sickness, disability, or old age. Most were chronically ill, aged widows. My mother called regularly upon these elderly women and organized her

Sunday school classes to visit them. She would take food to them, and on special occasions such as Christmas and Easter, she would enlist the family's help in loading up one or two in our "Sunday" car to take to them to church, where it sometimes took our entire family effort to help them hobble up the church steps.

Her greatest domestic pride other than her flowers was her cooking. She was locally famous for her culinary skills and especially for her homemade bread. She had gained much of her cooking know-how, including the art of baking home-made bread, from my father's sister Aunt Mot. My mother had spent a large part of World War II with my father's family while he was in the Pacific. Baking bread was an ancient tradition in my father's German farm community and a source of great pride among the women of the area.

Fried chicken was another delicacy that she prepared with expert skill. I played my own role in providing the chicken for Sunday dinner, when fried chicken was served each and every week of the year. I had done my part the day before by helping my father chase down a chicken for the dinner. I had aided in the land-bound bird's execution by tying the chicken by its legs upside down to the wooden cross bar of our outdoor clothesline, and I had brought the scalding water to pour over the still-flapping and bleeding body after my father had quickly cut its head off with his razor-sharp United States Army–issued pocketknife. The feathers that remained after the scalding had to be carefully plucked out by hand. The denuded carcass could then be presented to my mother for gutting, cleaning, and carving into various pieces for frying. She was careful to identify and save from the chicken's "innards" the liver, which was considered a special delicacy when fried. Attending to this less than tasteful task exempted me from any other kitchen duties on Sunday afternoon.

While my mother stayed on the farm during the early years of my life, she began to work part-time at my elementary school library when I was about nine years old. Within a few years, she graduated to a job at the county library. Because my mother felt she should read all of the current best-sellers so as to recommend or quietly censor them to the other church ladies who frequented the library, her experience as a librarian enriched our home. Many people would stop by the library to get a book recommendation or just to visit "Miss Lou" and gossip. For the latter pastime, the main sport of the community, the library served as the central source of information. She was active in the circles of church ladies who met on a regular basis to discuss subjects such as the missionary travels of St. Paul about the ancient world.

Like my father, she was a mixture of strict disciplinarian, humanitarian, and expert on every conceivable domestic aspect of farm home life. Also like my father, she was greatly respected and loved in the community. Everybody seemed to

know "Mr. George and Miss Lou." Raised a Baptist, she converted to Lutheranism when she married my father and
became a regular Sunday school teacher at the Lutheran
Church. Once selected "Women of the Year" for the county,
she was active in a variety of community activities such as
service clubs. She would give frequent talks on almost any
conceivable subject to the various community clubs in the
area. Her presentations might cover the best way to raise aza-
leas or pickle cucumbers, or she might review the most recent
book on the life of Eleanor Roosevelt.

The county's tiny public library was housed in a two-
story brick building known as Memorial Hall, originally
completed in about 1817 as the Pleasant Retreat Academy
for boys. It was the oldest building in the county and the historical nexus for the town. Five thousand Yankee cavalry soldiers passed through Lincolnton on April 20, 1865, under
the command of General John Palmer, just eleven days after
Lee surrendered his Army of Northern Virginia at
Appomattox. The blue-coated soldiers rode right by the
Academy and did not bother to burn it down. Primarily for-
aging for food for their return trip north, they had stopped
their scorched-earth tactic made popular by General
Sherman, since the war was considered essentially over. Thus,
courtesy of General Palmer, the Pleasant Retreat Academy
and Lincolnton itself were preserved in its antebellum state.

The brick structure, with its pine-paneled interior, was leased to the county by the United Daughters of the Confederacy. Holding in 1960 about eight hundred books, its bottom floor comprised the county's only public library. The upstairs consisted of a musty Confederate museum that was tightly closed to the public and used as a meeting place for the Daughters. After the library was closed for the day, I had complete access to the museum by going up the dark back stairs while my mother finished shelving books. The historic gems that could be found there included musty, old gray Confederate uniforms, displays of Confederate money, authentic Confederate flags brought back from battlefields of Virginia, rusted pistols and long rifles, and the letters of young Confederate soldiers written in the field. A number of these letters apparently had been removed from their dead bodies and sent back home to their families as a substitute for returning the bodies, which was impractical. The museum honored three Confederate generals who came from Lincoln County—Robert Johnston, Robert Hoke, and Stephen Dodson Ramseur, nicknamed "Dod." As a boy, Dod had graduated from Pleasant Retreat Academy. In his honor, the only school that Boyce and I would ever attend together was named General Stephen D. Ramseur High School, otherwise called Lincolnton High. Ramseur was the youngest West Point graduate to have served in the Confederate Army. Killed at the age of twenty-seven at the Battle of Cedar

Creek, Virginia, he came home in a wooden box by train and was buried in the cemetery of St. Luke's Episcopal Church Cemetery, not too far from my high school friend Sam Robinson. Sam, the valedictorian of our class, had been killed in an accident at his summer job at a cotton mill just a few weeks after our graduation.

Dod Ramseur was buried along by Sam under the shady, cool oaks of the Episcopal cemetery. As a boy, Dod was said to have ridden his snow sled down the hill upon which the shaded Academy was perched. When I was a boy, the painted portraits of Generals Ramseur and Hoke would stare down at me whenever I sneaked upstairs to explore the Confederate museum. The spirits of the Confederates seemed very much alive in the place, and I sensed their displeasure at my snooping about the museum's relics and some of their personal items.

The Pleasant Retreat Academy, which housed both the public library and the cloistered Confederate museum, served as the county's only historical repository for most of the twentieth century. One of the guardians of the museum was Frances Fair, the county librarian for whom my mother worked. Frances was an eccentric woman who had never married. She was tall and had pasty, white skin that hung from her body frame like a loose sheet. She always wore long dresses that I have concluded must have belonged at one time to her mother. The dresses had high, tight collars and reached to the floor, even in the heat of summer. A kind, quiet woman, she walked daily back and forth the four blocks between her home on West Main Street and the library. Keeping to herself, Frances's life seemed to revolve around the library and caring for her elderly, bedridden mother.

When I was a boy, Frances seemed ancient. The old family house where she lived with her mother seemed even more ancient. It had fallen into general disrepair, and the yard was overgrown with weeds. Frances's mother, Irva Reinhardt Fair, was both the daughter of a Confederate officer named Wallace M. Reinhardt and the great-granddaughter of the local pioneer Christian Reinhardt, owner of a tannery near Ramsour's Mill, the site of a locally famous Revolutionary War battle.

The fact that her maternal grandfather Wallace Reinhardt had served in the Civil War qualified Frances for immediate and unquestioned membership in the Daughters of the Confederacy. Frances's brother Victor Fair, a dedicated amateur historian of some skill, had recorded much of the county's early history, especially stories about the region during the American Revolution. In turn, Frances served as the guardian of the family archives and Victor Fair's precious historical records.

Victor Fair had written a short history of the county during the American Revolution days from stories he heard from his elderly grandfather, Wallace Reinhardt. When Wallace

Reinhardt was a boy in the early 1800s, many surviving, aged Revolutionary War veterans bemused themselves and others by recounting stories of those early frontier days and their war adventures.

From the windows of the Pleasant Retreat Academy, which stood at the peak of a prominent hill, you could look out and in the distance catch sight of the location of the Revolutionary Battle of Ramsour's Mill about a mile away. Collecting oral tradition from his grandfather, Victor Fair chronicled many unknown details about this obscure battle between loyalist Tories and the rebel Patriots fought just a short distance from the site of the old library on June 20, 1780.

Rarely discussed in history books, this battle was believed by some historians to be a turning point of the American Revolution. A small army of about twelve hundred loyalist colonial Tories had encamped just outside the present locale of Lincolnton by a grist mill owned by Diedrich Ramsour and the tannery owned by Christian Reinhardt, Frances and Victor Fair's great-great-grandfather.

I rummaged through Fair's unpublished little book *The Hills of Home* and became intrigued by it. I was particularly intrigued by the true story therein of two unlikely friends, a German frontiersman named Adam Reep and a slave known only as Fesso. Fair attributed the outcome of the Battle of Ramsour's Mill to the collaboration of these two men.

Johnson Wilson Blake (1906-1975)
Boyce's Father

Ruth Friday Blake "Miss Ruth" (1917-1998), Boyce's Mother

Untold Way in Georgetown

Miss Ruth with Boyce

JOHNSON BLAKE WITH BOOKER T. BLAKE, BOYCE'S UNCLE

BLAKE FAMILY PHOTOGRAPH
(HOLINESS CHURCH ON BLAKE PROPERTY IN FAR LEFT BACKGROUND)

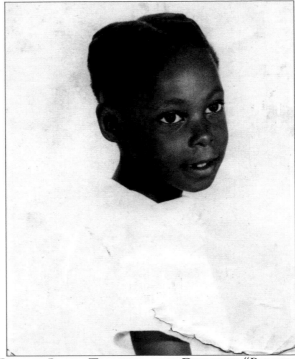

DONNA BLAKE TOLLIVER, THE DREADED "PUNKIN"
BOYCE'S YOUNGEST SISTER

ANNETTE JARRETT,
MISS MERRY CHRISTMAS COURT

RONNIE JOHNSON

Emmanuel Lutheran Church

George Stoudemire with local farmers

GEORGE A. STOUDEMIRE (1919-1982)
LINCOLN COUNTY AGRICULTURAL AGENT

PANORAMIC VIEW OF THE STOUDEMIRE FARM WITH THE SOUTH RANGE OF

Prize Show Cows,
Elsie and Missie

Heidi

the Blue Ridge Mountains in the background

LINCOLN COUNTY COURTHOUSE (1853)

MOORE'S CHAPEL A.M.E. ZION CHURCH, WHERE BOYCE'S GREAT-UNCLE, THE REV. HILLIARD BLAKE, PREACHED (1920-1924)

I became fascinated by the relationship of Reep and Fesso and their various adventures from the county's almost forgotten past. For reasons unknown, they had become fast friends before the war reached the Carolinas. On at least two occasions, Fesso had been kidnapped by thieving slave traders in the area. Known as "Catchers," they would steal slaves, then resell them in other parts of the country. Utilizing his knowledge of the backcountry, as well as sitings of Fesso reported to him by friendly Indians with whom he traded, Reep managed both times to track down Fesso's kidnappers and rescue him. Reep returned his friend Fesso to his master, a tanner by the name of Christian Reinhardt, and to Fesso's wife, Dinah.

The story of the friendship between Adam Reep and Fesso intrigued me for a number of reasons. I had spent a great deal of my childhood on the very site of the Battle of Ramsour's Mill near places where these two compatriots plotted against the Tories and the impending arrival of the invading British. In the early 1960s, the all-white middle school that I attended was built directly over the spot of some of the most intense fighting of the battle and was appropriately named Battleground School. At recess, I doubtless played tag and softball over unmarked graves of Tory and Patriot soldiers alike, atop the hill where the loyalists had made their battle encampment. Only a few stone markers commemorated the several hundred men killed there one foggy morning. The most prominent one ironically honored two Tory brothers killed there, "Nicholas and Philip Warlick—Loyal Servants of the King," as their stone marker was engraved. A football arena built next to the school also covered part of the battle scene and was duly named Battleground Stadium. It was on this playing field that Fox and I would one day have some of our own most glorious moments.

Reinhardt's tannery, where Fesso worked, was located near an encampment of Tories who had gathered to await the arrival of Cornwallis and his army on June 20, 1780. Victor Fair recorded that at great risk, Fesso had spied on the Tories for his friend Adam Reep. Fesso's owner Christian Reinhardt was reputed to be a Tory. Fesso relayed vital information to Reep about the number of Tory soldiers, their positions, and their supplies of munitions that proved critical to the Patriot farmers and frontiersmen who were outnumbered by five to one.

The Patriots launched a successful surprise early morning attack that turned into a rout as the fierce Scots-Irish mountaineers took out their long-standing wrath against the English on their Tory supporters. While Adam Reep became a local legend after the war, the fate of Fesso remains unknown. As slaves often took the names of their masters after they were freed, it is highly likely that descendants of Fesso remain in the area. In fact, I knew a few black families with the unlikely German last name of Reinhardt. Almost two centuries after Fesso lived, I am convinced that a classmate of Boyce and of mine by the name of Chyral Reinhardt is one of his descendants.

In later years, we found Mr. George Reinhardt, an elderly black man in his mid-80s who we believed was Fesso's great-great-grandson. He said Fesso's real Christian name was Festus. According to family lore, just before Fesso died, he requested to be buried on the top of the hill at Ramsour's Mill, but "not near any damned British or Hessians."

There was something I did not notice as a boy while absorbed in Victor Fair's accounts of Reep and Fesso among the dusty book stacks of the library where my mother worked. Until the 1960s, around the time my mother began to work there, a silent county policy dictated that blacks—with the exception of black school teachers—were not allowed to check out books. This was only one of the many examples of discrimination to which I was oblivious as a boy. While I never heard a racist or biased word out of the mouths of my parents, segregation was an accepted and unquestioned way of life.

It never occurred to me to ask my father why he never made calls on black farmers. I understand now that the vast majority of whites would not sell farmland to blacks. They preferred to keep them as sharecroppers and as sources of cheap labor. A few blacks had accumulated small plots of land, but only a very few owned enough land to form a self-supporting farm. Most blacks in the county either sharecropped land owned by white farmers, or they tended their own backyard gardens, where they grew vegetables to provide some food for the family. Like the Blakes, there might be room for a hog pen, and chickens could support themselves by scratching about for food on their own.

Just as the schools, churches, eating places, and drinking fountains were segregated, the industrial and farm economies were segregated, too. Blacks were largely denied jobs in the local mills. For black people, the only means for advancing their social and economic status was by joining the military or by going "up north" to find jobs in the integrated factories of Detroit or Cleveland.

Old times there are not forgotten, although presently, many people would prefer to forget those days, to pretend things were never as bad as they truly were for the blacks, or to cover up the days of slavery in southern plantation romanticism. While there was nothing romantic about the life of the Blakes, Fox and I, however, managed to carve out a few years of our boyhood where life seemed to be a sequence of card and softball games, punctuated by onerous Saturday workdays. Life was not exactly carefree, but time seemed to flow with a particular rhythm and regularity, and with the exception of picking up rocks for "that stupid well," we had more than our share of fun while it lasted.

Moonshine over Carolina

Everything good is on the highway.

—Ralph Waldo Emerson

Our farm and the black enclave of Georgetown, overlooked by Blake Hill, was surrounded by white rural folk who formed a major component of the southern culture from which Fox and I derived. Victory Grove Church (the "victory" was Christ's victory over death) was a small, well-scrubbed white wooden building that sat on a hill in a grove of hardwood trees beside a shaded little graveyard. The church's fundamentalist members were, by and large, local parishioners, most of whom lived within walking distance of the church.

During the week, the residents along Victory Grove Church Road were small-time farmers, or else they worked in the cotton mills and furniture plants; sometimes they did both. One industry that flourished in the area was more secretive, but not necessarily held in any less regard than farming or spinning cotton into yarn or making furniture. More than a few families who lived around us participated directly or indirectly in the illegal sale or production of beer or illegal liquor. During my childhood, Lincoln was one of the dry counties of North Carolina, where selling alcohol of any sort was illegal. Even by 1968, when I was eighteen, prohibition had not ended in Lincoln County.

At the time, the state of North Carolina was a patchwork of counties in which the sale of wine, liquor, or beer was a matter of local option and was either illegal or legal, depending on the wishes of the majority of voters in each county. Even in the more liberal urban centers, hard liquor could not be served "by the drink" in restaurants, but liquor bottles could be "brown-bagged," brought to the restaurant, and setups of ice, soda, or tonic water provided for an extra charge.

Secretive car runs from a dry to a wet county to buy liquor or beer were common among both adults and teenagers. In some counties, liquor was available from state-operated ABC (State Bureau of Alcohol Beverage Control) stores, where the sale of alcohol was controlled in order to collect tax revenues. In some counties, beer and wine could be purchased from grocery stores, but as a rule, roadside gasoline stations were the primary dispensaries of beer. Older teenagers could pull into a highway grocery store or gas station and literally fill up with both gasoline and beer, then barrel down the road often towards disaster.

One of the more hazardous consequences of this patchwork policy of illegal and legal selling of various types of alcohol was the beer run from a dry to a wet county by teenagers who would enlist the help of an older teenager of drinking age to buy alcohol for them. Many times, those making the trip would start drinking their booty on their triumphant trip home and end up plowing into a ditch, that is, if they were lucky. If less fortunate, the young drivers would run into a tree, telephone pole, or an oncoming car with the tragic, but not uncommon outcome, of multiple teenage fatalities.

Access to alcohol was intimately associated with automotive mobility. If the highway patrol spotted a car full of teenagers returning from the direction of a wet county line, suspicion was aroused, and chase was given. Most of the lawmen were wise enough to let themselves be outrun if the car did not stop at the sight of the ominous blue flashing lights. Most patrolmen understood that a high-speed chase could end in death over only a few six-packs of beer.

In Georgetown, these runs to the next county were unnecessary. Alcohol of all types was readily available

through local white bootleggers, an old term used for smug-
glers who hid some form of illegal contraband in their boots.
Bud Hester lived on the outskirts of Georgetown and was
one of the best-known, if not most-respected, bootleggers in
the area. The respect he earned was due to his bravado in
challenging the law and in asserting and supporting what
most people from pioneer days considered a natural human
right: to drink alcohol and thus find temporary release from
the pains of day-to-day life. In addition, Bud was a highly
visible member of his local church. The general assumption
prevailed that he got a wink and a nod from the local sheriff
as long as he did not sell homemade illegal whiskey, called
"moonshine," out his back door. Bud's operation was simple:
he resold in Lincoln County beer and whiskey he had bought
legally in a neighboring wet county. By providing alcohol
locally and thus reducing the number of runs for booze over
the county lines, Bud probably saved numerous teenage lives.

Bud Hester had customers black and white and applied
his usual markup of 100 percent to the cost of the booze he
sold, with the higher costs justified by the risks he assumed
in buying and transporting his goods from adjoining wet
counties. Additionally, Bud had to cover the costs involved in
paying off a corrupt sheriff's deputy now and then and in
paying his bail bond and fine in the case of a raid. When he
got caught, his fines were standard, easily payable, and his jail
stays lasted only a few months at most. They were reported

by Bud to be "no big deal," as he typically spent the prison time with old friends, while his federally insured, hard-earned profits went right on collecting interest at the local savings and loan institution.

The making and transporting of moonshine was a much riskier business than the reselling of beer and whiskey bought in wet counties. Several of the rural white families near our farm were still engaged in this ancient and honored domestic industry. As moonshine stills were scattered about our foothill county, most locals knew where it could easily be obtained. I was aware of the location of several operating stills within walking distance of our farm, one operated by the father of one of my white friends. For me to approach his family-owned still, however, was to risk being peppered with pellets from his father's shotgun.

Making moonshine was a highly skilled art, one that had been nurtured in the hills and mountains for two hundred years before my lifetime. Making good whiskey was a family tradition. My buddy could describe to me in great detail the techniques of his father's art.

The Appalachian mountaineer method of making alcohol from corn first began with transforming the starch of the grain, in this case corn, into sugar. More sophisticated distillers (hence the name "still," shortened from *distillery*) used malt for this purpose, but malt was rarely available to the mountaineers. Unground corn would be placed in a pot, generally made of copper, with a small hole or holes in the bottom. Warm water was poured over the corn, and a warm cloth placed over the top of the tub. As water dripped through the corn in the tub, more warm water would be added regularly to replenish the water that was slowly seeping out of the bottom of the tub. This process continued for three to seven days until the corn had sprouted and the sprouts were a few inches long. Although the chemistry of the process was unknown to the farmers managing it, enzymes in the germinating corn seeds served the same purpose that malt did for the more advanced distillers. The starch in the corn was gradually converted into sugar by enzymes in the germinating corn seeds.

Next, the sprouted corn was dried and ground into corn meal. The sweet meal was then made into corn mash by cooking it in boiling water for a few days. Ideally, this sweet corn mash was enhanced by the addition of rye malt, which made it more flavorful. This step, however, was not an indispensable part of the process. If fermentation had begun, yeast, if available, was added to hasten the process. If yeast was not available, the fermentation process would take significantly longer, and the mash had to stand for eight to ten days. It was essential to carefully track its temperature, a task that required constant attention, even in the moonlight. Once this step was completed, the sugar of the mash, which was now "sour," had been converted into carbonic acid and alcohol. The resulting concoction was alternately referred to as the "wash," or "beer," but its sourness made it generally unfit for human consumption. (Excess or unfit wash was often used as pig slop and resulted in mildly euphoric hogs stumbling about in their pens.)

Suitable corn wash, or beer, would be placed in the still, a vessel with a closed head connected to a spiral tube called the "worm." It was the worm that would cause the ultimate downfall of the industry when distillers began to use the coils of old car radiators for this part of the distilling process.

The worm was wrapped by a heavy cloth jacket through which cold water constantly passed over, hence the need to locate the distillery close to a stream. As a wood fire is built under the vessel, the "spirits" of the alcohol rose in the vapor along with the steam. In the cooled worm, the alcohol spirits condensed and trickled into pots, jars, or tubs. This first brew would be relatively crude and had to be redistilled to rid it of any residual water and impurities that would detract from the smoothness of the distillate. The liquor from the second distilling was commonly known as the "doublings" because it was distilled twice and therefore was purer and smoother to drink. The final step was to run the now-pure liquor, or grain alcohol, through charcoal filters of one sort or another to get rid of other impurities. For quality control when completed, the moonshine was ready for "tasting," otherwise known as "sipping," always by the proprietor.

No moonshiner would think of selling his product if he was not willing to drink it himself. If found to be acceptable, the liquor was then prepared for shipping out in special cars.

The more advanced art of whiskey making involved aging the 'shine in oak barrels. This was generally not the practice of the Carolina moonshiners, however, since one had to move the finished product rapidly in this part of the world before the local sheriff found the still, or before one was reported by a feuding neighbor, a local competitor, an overzealous Baptist preacher, or sometimes an angry, bitter ex-wife.

The finished crystal-clear product was referred to as "moonshine" mainly because most of its production and transportation took place in secrecy at night when the Carolina moon would shine favorably upon the farmer's furtive work. The 'shine, or "mountain dew," was typically sold in either pint- or quart-sized glass containers with the brand names Mason or Ball. Normally, these jars were used by farmers' wives to store vegetables and fruit for the winter and were so common, particularly in my agricultural community, that they provided a good disguise for their colorless contents. The use of fancy or unique labels was unwise, since they might be traced. The brand-name jar, however, added a certain cachet to the product, and these famous canning jars became the favorite containers for moonshine. Even as an amateur, I would have suspicions about the origin, quality, and purity of the moonshine if it was stored in anything other than a Ball or Mason jar.

The finest product was nearly 200 proof, meaning it was 100 percent alcohol. A little could go a long way. A few gulps would hit you like lightning; hence, the name "white lightning" was usually given to the potent substance. Like general anesthesia, the effect was almost immediate when a dose of the agent was administered rapidly. A large amount imbibed too quickly by a novice consumer could lead to disastrous results.

Making whiskey was still considered by many to be an inviolable personal right, in which the government had no business interfering, much less taxing the product. The tradition of making home brew dated all the way back to the Scots-Irish and German ancestors of the local population. The Scots-Irish, in particular, had strong antigovernment attitudes derived from their ingrained fear of being controlled by a distant, historically English government that could intrude upon their right to regulate themselves according to the wishes of the local clan. They typically believed the main purpose of government was to fight wars when needed and perhaps to provide roads and schools that would be locally operated and controlled without any "damn government bureaucracy."

In Lincoln County, the making and selling of illegal whiskey resembled a cat-and-mouse game between the local

makers and distributors of moonshine and the county sheriff, who was duty-bound by the law and by the Baptist
preachers to oppose the making, transportation, and selling
of alcohol. Most people enjoyed hearing and talking about
the most recent contest of wills between the sheriff, who, for
the better part of my boyhood, was the affable, well-liked,
regularly re-elected Harvin Crouse, and a particular group of
irascible bootleggers who considered Harvin to be their
nemesis. The most recent discovery of a backwoods moonshine operation always made the front page of the *Lincoln
Times* and was usually accompanied by a picture of Sheriff
Crouse with axe raised to come crashing down on the shame-
faced, handcuffed proprietor's still. Sometimes Sheriff
Crouse would haul off the remnants of the destroyed still to
put on display in front of the county courthouse as a demonstration that he was "tough on the moonshiners" and to get
the Baptist preachers temporarily off his back.

Whenever a vote came up to allow liquor sales in the
county, it was defeated. Sheriff Crouse once privately told my
father that Lincoln County would remain dry as long as the
local bootleggers and the Baptist preachers could get those
loyal to them to the polls to vote against making it legal.

There was one classic moonshine story in Lincoln
County that was unforgettable. It was the story of Miss
Mattie Reep and of how she "got the goat" of Sheriff Crouse
in her own resourceful way. While I had heard bits and pieces

of the story growing up, I learned some of the finer details of the story from Sheriff Barbara Pickens, my childhood friend from church. Barbara was the first and only female sheriff ever elected to that office in the history of North Carolina. I had not seen her in over thirty years when, on a visit home, I decided on impulse to stop by the sheriff's office, then housed in an old grammar school building at an intersection occupied by the Pleasant Retreat Academy on one corner and Drum's Funeral Home on another. The female deputy posted at the front desk was polite when I informed her that I was an old friend of Sheriff Pickens, that I wanted to speak to her if she had the time, and that I wasn't sure she would even remember me. The deputy excused herself and retired to a back office. In a few moments, I heard a loud exclamation of delight, and suddenly the imposing figure of Sheriff Pickens emerged from the office with badge, gun, and all. "Why, Alan Stoudemire, I haven't seen you in years!"

The next thing I knew, I found myself engulfed by her strong arms in a big, warm hug. It was as if her beloved brother had just returned alive from a far-off war. There are few places in the world where one might be lucky enough to experience that kind of welcome, much less from your local sheriff. Before long, we were talking about old times at our Lutheran church, the oldest church in town, the original structure having been built after the Revolution by the tanner Christian Reinhardt with the help of war hero Adam Reep in 1785. After reviewing the series of Lutheran preachers who had come and gone since I had left home, I asked her if the stories about Miss Mattie and Barbara's predecessor Sheriff Harvin Crouse were really true. With deputies and office personnel gathered around to find out what all the commotion was about and then intrigued by the tale of Miss Mattie, this is what Sheriff Barbara Pickens told me.

Miss Mattie was a local seller of pint-sized Mason jars of moonshine, which proved to be her only source of hard cash after her farmer husband had passed away. They had no children, so Miss Mattie lived alone down a long dirt road not far from the area of Bootleg Hill, which, of course, was well known to me. Her many friends and neighbor allies would warn her on her new telephone whenever they saw a sheriff's car approaching. Miss Mattie was served with search warrants once or twice a year, but no liquor was ever found in her house or on her land. It was, nevertheless, common knowledge in Lincoln County that the 'shine she sold was "safe and smooth." Sheriff Crouse had made only feeble efforts to catch Miss Mattie, as he knew she likely could not pay a court fine, and it was unthinkable that this generally honest country lady, a regular attendee at her local Church of God, could possibly spend even one night in jail.

Things had begun to sour in the moonshine market because of the recent appearance of "bad 'shine." Several deaths had occurred in Lincoln County from drinking illegal liquor, and these fatal intoxications were increasing in frequency. The nearly harmless cat-and-mouse game with the distillers had become a serious problem due to an unidentified lethal toxin that was contaminating certain batches of moonshine. To make matters worse, it was tasteless and could not be detected by even the most experienced sipper. Sheriff Crouse became motivated to stop the trafficking of illegal whiskey until the problem could be diagnosed and remedied.

Doctors at the state university medical school in Chapel Hill, who were studying the situation, discovered that the bad 'shine contained lead, that imbibing the tainted liquor could result in kidney failure, brain damage, and even death, as Lincoln County folks had already learned. It did not take long for experts to trace the source of this poisonous lead to several captured stills in the area. Enterprising moonshiners had taken coils out of old car radiators to make the "worm" of the still, the wired, coiled component that arose out of their distilling apparatus. Many of the old, rusty car radiator coils had joints that were soldered together with lead, which would dissolve into the liquor as the steam went through the coil in the distilling process. Thus, toxic batches of 'shine were being produced with varying degrees of lead concentration. A new effort in the interest of the public health of the county and state was made to close down the industry, at least until word could get around to the moonshiners about the danger of their using radiator coils. Even then, however, there was no telling whether these midnight distillers would change their methods. Additionally, poisonous moonshine could be brought from out of state. Sheriff Crouse could no longer wink at even Miss Mattie's involvement in the trade.

The secret to Miss Mattie's invulnerability was that first, she had an early warning system, and second, before the deputies could reach her house, she would toss the moonshine out her back door or drop the filled Mason jars down her well. Sheriff Crouse believed he had figured out the reason he and his deputies were never successful in finding evidence in her house. Reports of the odd, strong odor of her well water in the backyard were more than a little suspicious. Given the public health threat from lead-containing moonshine, Miss Mattie had to be shut down.

The well-meaning sheriff had a plan. Right before dusk, long before his deputies were to head down the dirt road to her house, Sheriff Crouse would sneak through the woods, crawl under her back porch with a large, deep, and wide pan, and wait to catch any moonshine Miss Mattie might try to pour out. With just enough daylight left to see and befriend Mattie's hound dog, Blue, he would quietly whistle for the dog and seduce him with meat and bones. As soon as it became dark, he would proceed cautiously to the porch and wait beneath to catch the evidence of Miss

Mattie's contraband at the same time his deputies knocked on the door to serve the search warrant. Thus, the trap would be set.

Sure enough, the plan went well, and on cue, he was hiding under her porch with his new friend Blue literally eating out of his hand. While under her house, he noticed another secret to Miss Mattie's success. She had a hole cut in her living room floor, obviously, he surmised, for the purpose of dumping the moonshine in the event that the back door happened to be covered by deputies.

Sheriff Crouse heard Miss Mattie moving about the house. Several minutes before the predetermined time for his deputies to arrive with the search warrant, Miss Mattie's telephone rang several times, followed by a scurry of activity, the sounds of her slippered feet shuffling quickly back and forth between her back door and what he guessed was a centrally located interior room where she kept her liquor hidden. Miss Mattie's emergency procedures were quick and efficient.

Then something happened that Sheriff Crouse had not counted on. The back porch light came on. Miss Mattie pushed back the screen door, which opened wide onto the porch under which Crouse crouched, and she began calling for Blue, who ordinarily could smell the law a mile away. Blue appeared dutifully with a large, new bone in his mouth. Miss Mattie became suspicious. Through the rough, worn wood-plank slatting of her porch floor, her sharp eyes caught the glint of the sheriff's badge and his shiny pan. It did not take her long to figure that she had been set up, that Blue had been bribed, and that she had a lawman hiding right under her feet.

Sheriff Pickens reported that at that point, Miss Mattie loudly announced, "Well, Blue, that damned old bladder infection is about to cause me to break loose. I don't think I can hold it any longer! 'Scuse me, Blue." With that announcement, she positioned herself directly above the gleaming badge of Sheriff Crouse and relieved herself. To the sheriff's horror and disgust, he found himself spitting and wiping Miss Mattie's urine off his face and hair. In the meantime, Miss Mattie had once again dispensed of her modest few jugs and jars down the well.

As she headed back up the few short steps to her house, she paused and shouted to the sheriff, who was still underneath the house, "Why, Sheriff, for the Lord's sake, I can't believe you're such a damned pervert so as to go hiding under a widow's porch to try to look up her dress! This is about the most disgustin' thing I ever heard of! Why, by God, I might just have to press charges. At the least, I'm gonna' call your preacher up at the Baptist Church where you have the nerve to teach Sunday school!"

Feigning utter disgust at him and barely able to restrain herself from bursting into laughter, she finished her indignant march up the steps and slammed the back door.

Sheriff Crouse beat a hasty retreat into the woods with Blue naively trotting along behind him expecting more bones. The sheriff refused to let his deputies see him humiliated in this manner.

Miss Mattie graciously opened the front door to the deputies and greeted them in a friendly manner, "Hello there, boys. You must be looking for Sheriff Crouse. After y'all get finished lookin' through the house, you'll find him and Blue out in the back woods doing God knows what!" She could contain herself no longer. To the deputies' befuddlement, she collapsed in hysterical laughter to the floor, where she pounded her fists in convulsive delight.

To bring the moonshine out of the hills and mountains down to local distribution centers, cars had to be rigged with special tanks. Old Fords and Chevrolets were generally the vehicles of choice because their bubble-shaped trunks could accommodate the tanks. New cars were not used because they were prone to be wrecked or rammed by the law. Modifying the trunk of the car to haul whiskey was simple enough when steel barrels became available. Simple spouts could be installed for draining the 'shine into the local distributors' waiting pots or even large twenty-gallon milk cans, which were excellent not just for storage, but also for innocently hiding about a farm.

The real danger and excitement occurred when a runner was fully loaded and ready to move the liquor down to local distributors in the lower Carolinas through the mountain "thunder" roads, so named because of the loud rumble of the engines of the powerful moonshine-laden race cars. It was critical not to be noticed, chased, or stopped by the local sheriff, or worse yet, by federal agents referred to as "revenuers." The federal government's main concern about the illegal production of alcohol was that taxes could not be collected on it. One technique used by the runners to escape detection was to add to the vehicle's rear some extra shock absorbers, which kept the car on an even keel so as to avoid the telltale sign of a weighted-down trunk reflecting a full, heavy load of liquid contraband.

The federal agents had little interest in the moral dimensions of the liquor business. That was a matter for the fundamentalist preachers. By the 1950s, almost all of America realized that the right to drink liquor could be neither suppressed nor eliminated, as the Prohibition disaster of the 1920s had proven. Busting stills and chasing down moonshiners was more a matter of adding tax money to the federal and state coffers.

It was almost inevitable that a runner would sometimes be spotted or would encounter a roadblock, since it was not hard for a lawman to see or hear the powerful engines of the professional moonshine runners. Their cars, like those of their NASCAR descendants, were supercharged by the addition of extra carburetors and by souping up the engine in order to make them run faster and longer than the prosaic cars of the average county sheriff. The wiser sheriffs learned that trying to eliminate the production and sale of moonshine was all but a waste of time. As soon as one still was raided and busted and the proprietor fined and given a short jail sentence, another still would begin operating to fill the vacuum in the local market. Also, the tried and convicted moonshiner soon would be out of jail and rebuilding another still deeper in the woods.

In most cases, the county sheriff was cautious in a chase, since the moonshiners often tossed nails out of the window to puncture their pursuer's tires, or they would pull a latch that would release oil onto the highway, usually as they were rounding a curve. The pursuing officer soon would be skidding into an oak tree or ditch or careening down a mountain ravine. Also, the moonshine runners rigged their cars with detachable rear bumpers so that if the police rammed them from the rear, the bumper would release and be run over by the lawman's car. The result, as intended, was a blown tire or loss of control of the car in pursuit. There was no reason for anyone to die just for making and running moonshine, especially since the sheriff and his deputies were often friends of the moonshiners and their relatives in the small counties of western Carolina. Lawmen and moonshiners knew each others' kinfolk.

The "outsider" federal agents were more aggressive, had no local ties to the culprits or their families, and were feared because their aggressive pursuits were dangerous for all involved. Sometimes federal agents showed up to "clean up the county," especially when they surmised that the local sheriff was too tolerant or "on the take" from local distillers or distributors.

To confuse matters for both the local law and the federal agents, the moonshine runners on occasion would take great fun in calling the sheriff's office to inform him in a disguised voice that there was going to be "a run of moonshine" through a specific route at a specific time on a specific night. The runner would make a dry run (without any liquor or even a pistol or shotgun on board) for the pure pleasure of taunting the law and for the pride of outrunning the law in his newly supercharged Ford, Chevy, or Plymouth.

The runner was always careful to remove the license tag from the car and to place it face down in his rearview window, so if caught, he could claim his tag had "just fallen down." Then the driver would run the route at the appointed time and, with great delight and at speeds over one hundred miles per hour, blow by staked-out police officers hidden alongside roads. Before the police were able to start their engines and pull their cars onto the road, the dry runner was already at least a mile down the highway, and the chase was on. The runner would choose a route he knew well, one with many dirt roads and hiding places available for an escape in case the law seemed to be closing in on him. More often than not, the runner would slow down just enough to create the illusion that he might be catchable, then speed up again, soon losing the lights of justice in their rearview mirror and wondering whether the law had "spun out" or landed in a ditch. In the event that a roadblock had been set up along the way, the worst offense with which he could be charged was speeding. Roadblocks were rare because the sheriff knew that the crazier boys would try to run through or around them, that their front bumpers were reinforced with steel just for that purpose. Only the federal agents would risk the possibility of a fatality—their own or that of a runner—over moonshine.

The Scots-Irish farmers stirring the corn mash by night and worshiping God on Sunday morning were fiercely independent. They loved the freedom they had found in the Carolina hills, and, as invading British General Cornwallis had learned in 1780, they were not going to give up their God-given freedoms without a fight. And so, continuing the tradition, the business of making, selling, and drinking alcohol was privately considered a God-given freedom along Victory Grove Church Road.

The running of moonshine would give birth to one of America's favorite sports. Racing stock cars was more than a sport in the South. It enjoyed nearly cult status. Richard Petty ranked only slightly below Robert E. Lee as a southern hero. Petty's racing car, the famous Number 43, was a cultural icon to be given all due reverence. The moonlight drag racing of cars whose engines were specially modified to outrun the local sheriff on a run of illegal whiskey would eventually develop over the years into the NASCAR racing circuit, where the idols of the South, like Petty, would be worshiped at such holy public temples as the Charlotte Motor Speedway.

The moonshine culture consisted of rebellious country folk, a shady distribution network, and the master mechanics who built and serviced the engines of the runners. Two families who lived along Victory Grove Church also lived along the edge of the law. The families were rumored to drink heavily and held a reputation for violent domestic fights. They were the Pratt family and the Farmer family. Between them, they supplied several generations of bullies to the local schoolyards and encounters of various kinds with the law. I dreaded riding the county school bus that ran by the end of the dirt road leading into our property because I was one of those bullied by the older Pratt boys.

Rumor had it that the oldest of the Pratt boys, Jimmy, would get into violent arguments with his drunkard father, who had no obvious source of employment. The arguments were provoked by the elder Pratt's beating the mother and the younger children. There was little doubt that the Pratt children were abused and consequently vented their rage on the children at the playground and on the school bus. I knew that I would be beaten to a pulp and possibly even cut with a hidden rusty pocketknife, standard issue for the Pratts, if I dared to fight back.

The Pratts were tough. Even as young teenagers, they were known for their drinking. They followed in a well-established family tradition. It was assumed that old man Pratt got his money and his liquor somewhere along the moonshine distribution network.

The Farmers were a different sort of family. Beside their house, they operated a spare parts business, a junkyard for old cars from which spare parts were cannibalized for resale. They also ran a garage in their backyard for repairing any make and model of American car. Near their house was an old abandoned school bus, which at times appeared to house members of the family or their visiting relatives. You could never be sure. The Farmers were known for their expertise in modifying cars for racing, otherwise known as "souping them up." In the midnight drag races up and down Victory Grove Road, the Farmers' car almost always won. Johnny Farmer, who was the oldest of the crew, had an Elvis-like persona and was recognized as "the King" of Victory Grove Church Road. He possessed Elvis's good looks, smoothness, and charm and was known for more than his racing and fighting skills; few country girls left the back seat of his legendary 1957 Chevrolet with their virtue completely intact.

Johnny's younger brother Frankie took a liking to me for some reason and would shield me on the school bus from Eddie Pratt whenever Eddie's violent tendencies became excessive. Since Frankie was the brother of Johnny, no one dared to mess with Frankie. The Farmer family members stuck together, and everyone knew it. Frankie was smaller than Johnny, but he was a quick and nimble fighter. Also, Eddie Pratt knew that Frankie often carried a knife, which, in dire circumstances, could quickly compensate for his small physical stature. And so, whenever Frankie was around, I felt relatively safe.

I wished many times that the school bus was integrated because any of the Blakes would have helped me out with Eddie Pratt. We stuck together. Instead, I stayed close to Frankie Farmer whenever possible. I rode the bus only when my father could not drop me off at school on the way to his office at the courthouse. I never told my father about my troubles with Eddie Pratt. I was twelve years old.

There was little contact between the blacks in Georgetown and the whites on Victory Grove Church Road. On more than one occasion, I heard Miss Ruth and Johnson Blake refer to the Pratts and the Farmers and tell their children to "watch out for those white boys because they're tied up with the liquor business and Bud Hester." The Blakes were well aware of their proclivity to drink heavily and to resolve family conflicts by physical fighting.

The principal area of contact between the rural black and white worlds was through alcohol and cars. The Blake brother who was counterpart and competitor to Johnny Farmer was none other than Johnny Blake. Johnny had obtained a souped-up Ford of his own. From hearsay, I learned that Johnny Farmer and Johnny Blake had "had words" and that a challenge had been issued for a race between Johnny Blake's Ford and Johnny Farmer's Chevy. If I were to place a bet, and if Fox were to place a bet, although he was opposed to the practice of gambling and reluctant to bet against his own brother, we would have laid all our money on Farmer's car. That's what we said to each other anyway. Fox and I knew what a moonshine car could do. If Johnny Farmer was not an actual moonshine runner, he certainly worked on suspicious-looking cars in his backyard garage. Another suspicious clue observed by some of the older Blakes was the close eye the sheriff seemed to keep on the Farmers' property at night. What was ironic was that, other than the color of their skin, these two rivals for bragging rights between Georgetown and the Victory Grove Road were more alike than different.

Johnny was next to the oldest of the Blake brothers and was known for fast cars and fast women, of whom he usually had more than one, and for the pistol he sometimes carried in the pocket of his black leather jacket. Johnny Blake was built like a brick, made of solid muscle, and liked to take more than one drink. He was a good friend of Bud Hester.

Johnny Blake could hit a softball farther than anyone in Georgetown. He established a local record of sorts when he hit a ball that sailed so far along the pasture that it actually rolled down the quarter-of-a-mile-long hill through the woods and ended its journey at the bottom of the creek. I remember because I was the one sent to retrieve the ball, and I managed to trap it before it was carried downstream. Had I lost it, the game would have ended, because we had no extras. I took pride in emerging from the woods with the muddy ball held high over my head, long after Johnny had leisurely rounded the bases and received congratulations at home plate.

Johnny loved a good time, and in spite of his tendency to kid me about my lack of experience with women and my "pitiful" skills in bid whiz, which he compared to the likely size of my genitals, I knew Johnny liked me. He would come immediately to my aid if he ever witnessed my being bullied by Jimmy or Eddie Pratt, and he always seemed glad to see me.

The day chosen for the great race between the two Johnnies was predictable. On the Sunday afternoon closest to their wedding anniversary, Johnson Blake would always take Miss Ruth somewhere special, usually to a nice black restaurant in Charlotte thirty miles away, the closest real city. They would leave soon after the Sunday morning church service, and they would be gone for the duration of the afternoon.

Around three o'clock that Sunday, the two Johnnies and their respective black and white entourages gathered. From the Victory Grove area came the rest of the Farmer male siblings, all of the Pratt brothers, the Plonck brothers, and ten or so curious and somewhat suspicious-looking white visitors, customers of Johnny Farmer's garage, I supposed. The Blake brothers were there, along with the Georgetown crowd who had played ball together for years, including Johnny Wayne Dorsey, Sylvester and Linton Cansler, Walter Sherrill, Frankie Moore, Ronnie Johnson, and myself. No animosity existed between the opposing groups, only good-natured, friendly kidding and general "cuttin' up," with the common hope on both sides that Miss Ruth would not arrive home prematurely for Sunday night church services.

In day-to-day life, however, the two worlds, black and white, were galaxies apart and generally indifferent to each other. The bridges that I had naively, unconsciously constructed with Georgetown had not been built by the other whites. On the other hand, respect for Johnson and Ruth Blake seemed universal.

A section of the pasture fence was removed temporarily to allow the two cars to enter. A track about a quarter mile in circumference was laid out with large rocks and sticks we stuck in the ground at the corners among the grass, brush, and small scrub pine. It was agreed that the race would consist of twenty laps. The two Johnnies exchanged good-natured jibes, then shook hands. As they revved up their engines, I felt exhilarated, but fearful, as well. It occurred to me that the great event that had generated such a high degree of anticipation and excitement would involve a significant element of danger. I quickly dismissed these useless, aggravating thoughts. The two groups of onlookers—one black, one white—maintained a distance from one another. The outcome of the race could determine bragging rights in the communities for years to come.

When the hand of a designated member of the group fell, the race would begin. Because I was recognized as a mutually agreeable and generally trustworthy person, as well as someone to blame for starting it if they got caught, it was my hand they chose. I raised, then lowered my arm, and the kings of Georgetown and Victory Grove Road were off in a cloud of dust and spewing small rocks. The long-anticipated race had begun.

The cars sped round and round the pasture, crushing rocks, weeds, and piles of manure. Both groups stood a respectful space back from the edge of the track. Dust first enveloped the cars, then the track, then us. The lead changed from time to time, but it was clear that, as Fox and I had predicted, Farmer was getting to the curbs quicker, claiming the inside lane, and pulling out ahead of Blake until he had almost a full half-lap lead going into the final five laps, which were loudly counted off in unison by the audience.

But then something terrible happened that we could not believe. Johnny Farmer, who seemed to have grown over-confident and reckless, suddenly flipped his car in a far turn. The car rolled over and over at least four times, enshrouded in dust, smoke, and what appeared to be several brief bursts of flame coming out of the hood. The car rolled down the pasture's incline into deep brush. A sudden chill fell over the black and white onlookers. I feared that Johnny must be dead; that an ambulance, along with Sheriff Crouse, would have to be called whether he was dead or alive; that our parents would find out; that the local paper would cover the story; and that there would be trouble and beatings for everyone involved. Miss Ruth would have every excuse to really "tear up some hide" this time. Johnny Blake had pulled his car over. Instead of enjoying his victory by default, he climbed out of his car in stunned disbelief, temporarily paralyzed like we were, as if waiting to shake off a bad dream.

Through the dirty cloud, we could scarcely make out the car at the far edge of the pasture among a group of tall and now crushed weeds and briars near the woods. Nobody moved. None of us wanted to be the first to see Johnny Farmer's mangled and lifeless body. As the veil of dust and smoke cleared, however, just like on Easter morning when Jesus emerged from his tomb, Johnny Farmer crawled out of the front passenger window without a visible scratch, and was so cool that, as he slowly walked around the car to survey the damage, he actually pulled a comb out of his hair and nonchalantly smoothed it back. It had been badly tousled in the wreck.

Without asking any assistance from the disbelieving crowd, he walked to the far side of the car and, with seemingly superhuman strength, he flipped it over on its wheels. He then climbed back into the car through the same window, started it easily, and drove through the pasture toward our joyous group. We believed we had witnessed a modern-day miracle. More than a few of us, both black and white, tossed a look of thanks over to the church at the edge of the pasture. Thank you, Jesus!

Johnny stopped the car just long enough to shake Johnny Blake's relieved hand, and with big grins on both their faces, Farmer mumbled, "I'll get you next time, Blake." What we had witnessed was not a miracle of God, but a miracle of Johnny Farmer's ability to reinforce his car with steel bars so that in the event his car flipped in a chase with the law, only a load of moonshine would be lost. As he drove away, he entered into the world of myth and legend, achieving on that Sunday afternoon in a scrub pasture in the Carolina foothills what so many men have sought: immortality in the memory of his people.

Under the Apple Tree and Black Angels

> We are escorted on every hand through life by spiritual agents, and a beneficent purpose lies in wait for us.
>
> —Ralph Waldo Emerson

As Fox and I grew into our teenage years together, we shared much in common. We were both aspiring athletes, we loved to play ball of any sort, and we were more or less committed to clean living. Several of the older Blake brothers, like Johnny, were somewhat less committed to clean living. They were committed, instead, to introducing the younger Blakes and me to some of the ways of the real world. I believe they considered this education part of their responsibility as older brothers.

Learning how to take a drink properly was a rite of initiation into manhood. While Fox maintained his policy of complete abstinence from alcohol and tobacco, his brother Sam and I were curious enough just to have a taste of the wicked stuff. I constantly begged Johnny to let me taste some 'shine the next time he had some on hand.

The opportunity came one summer afternoon when the whole Blake clan had gathered about to play bid whiz. Present were the older Blake brothers Frank and Tom, as well as Johnny. Given the crowd assembled that Saturday afternoon, and given that Johnny Wayne Dorsey, Sylvester Cansler, and Walter Sherrill from down the road in Georgetown (actually down a small dirt path that cut through a field and led to their houses) had shown up, as well, two simultaneous games were being conducted on card tables brought from the house and set up under the apple tree in the Blakes' backyard. Frank and Johnny, well into their twenties, no longer lived in the Blake house. By this time, Johnny was married. It occurred to me that it was unusual to have all the brothers together at once, unless it was a special event.

Each of the Blake brothers had his own distinct personality, strengths, and weaknesses. The oldest, Bob, was long gone from home. As he was almost ten years older, I barely knew him. Frank, the next oldest, was friendly and full of fun most of the time. He did not participate in Johnny's unrelenting jokes about my card-playing ability and lack of

knowledge about, and experience with, women. Frank, however, had a volatile temper that could be ignited with only
a small amount of alcohol acting as a trigger. I remember
vividly one summer day several years before when trouble
between these two older Blake brothers exploded.

Our dogs began to bark frantically, unusual for them
unless they sensed some sort of danger. I remember my
mother calling out to my father, "Oh, Lord, George, here
comes Frank Blake with a rifle, and he looks upset. Those
dogs know Frank, and I don't know why they would be
barking at him otherwise." My father also knew Frank well
and was familiar, too, with Frank's hair-trigger temper.
Perhaps because of his experience as a military officer, my
father somehow sensed that he was frightened and in some
kind of trouble, but not dangerous to us. It was inconceivable that he would present any danger to my family.
Besides, my father probably could have handled Frank
under almost any circumstances. Frank, Stewart, and my
father had worked a lot together on the farm in the past,
and they liked each other.

My mother, on the other hand, was obviously alarmed.
She knew that no man, black or white, carried a rifle in the
woods at dark for any legitimate reason, unless they were
heading home after a day's hunt. Frank was headed away
from home, and she could see something frightening in his
countenance and his frantic pace as he approached our house.

My father walked quickly, yet calmly to the back door. The rest of us were told to wait in a back room of the house until he saw what was the matter with Frank. My anxious mother, sister, and I waited as we heard soft and mumbled talking coming from the back porch and what sounded like Frank's crying, which mystified us even more.

My father soon appeared, carefully carrying the rifle with a towel wrapped about it, and announced to our shock and disbelief that "Frank and Johnny got into a fight over some girl, and Frank shot Johnny. I don't know how bad off Johnny is, or even if he's still alive. He's been taken to the hospital, and Frank wants me to take him to the sheriff's office, so he can turn himself in. He seems scared to death. I can put in a good word for Frank with Harvin Crouse. He probably lost his temper, like he can do. He went too far this time."

I watched my father put the rifle into the trunk of our family Chevrolet while Frank waited for him in the front seat. My father had put on his coat and tie to formalize the event. He drove off with Frank and was gone most of the evening. When he returned, he explained that Frank's fight with Johnny had started over Johnny's unwelcome show of affection toward Frank's girlfriend. The details of the confrontation were not clear, but apparently, Johnny had gotten the better of Frank in a fistfight, and Frank, refusing to be humiliated, had found his father's rifle, used until now only for squirrel hunting. He returned to shoot his stunned and disbelieving brother in the back, as Johnny ran for cover.

My father explained that Frank was in jail, that Johnny was in the hospital but would likely be all right, and that he would help Frank find a lawyer. We knew that Frank had more to fear from his parents than from the justice system.

As it turned out, Frank was convicted on a relatively minor charge, and he got off with a light sentence, because the incident was considered primarily a family squabble. Even Johnny was a somewhat sympathetic witness for his brother. Given my father's standing in the community, his serving as a character witness for Frank undoubtedly helped his case, as well. The bullet had lodged near the vertebrae in Johnny's spinal column. It was considered too risky to remove, so the doctors left the bullet in place. Johnny healed up fine with only a sore back and a constant reminder to stay away from Frank's girlfriends.

Once Frank's short sentence was completed and he returned home, Johnny's infringement on his brother's romantic turf ceased abruptly. A truce was declared between the two brothers, and all was forgiven, but not exactly forgotten. The most significant result that I observed from the incident is that they were no longer partners in our bid whiz games.

Johnny was known for his wily ways with women, but this was the first time he had been shot over his proclivities for the opposite sex. He was built strong and quick with both his wit and with his feet on the playing field, regardless of the game. He loved to carouse in our lively card games and knew just where to find a can of beer on a hot day. He was known not just for his good humor, but for his fighting ability. Most people knew better than to mess with Johnny Blake.

Johnny's reputation gave the Blakes special status in Georgetown. I, too, frequently mentioned his name and claimed, rightly so, that I was a friend of Johnny Blake, which provided not just special prestige, but also a certain degree of insurance against any playground bully, white or black. It also guaranteed that Bud Hester would sell me a cold can of beer at a fair bootlegged price.

Sam, a year older than Fox and me, was the most sensitive and fragile of the Blake brothers. He was prone to break into tears when he was tackled hard or landed on a rock in the pasture. Such instances would bring about immediate accusations from his brothers that he was "a mama's boy." Crying was not tolerated on the playing field, regardless of the nature of the injury. I remember one time when we were playing "hardball" with a real baseball, which we rarely used because there were not enough gloves to go around for everybody. Fox was hit in the face by a hard-driven ball. Only twelve or so at the time, Fox had broken briefly into tears. I was amazed to see that across the field, Sam was crying, too, perhaps harder than Fox. At the time, it was a matter of amusement. Later, it would represent to me their sharing of each other's pain, whether from hard-hit baseballs or from life itself.

It was ironic that Sam would see the most vicious combat in Vietnam and would become most traumatized by it. Like Johnny, however, Sam carried the same good-natured sense of humor and fun that seemed a fundamental family characteristic. Along with Fox and me, Sam formed the third musketeer in my father's dreaded Saturday work crews about the farm, as well as in our dam-building projects up and down the creek. It was Sam who I convinced at least once to smoke rabbit tobacco with me when Fox had wisely refused.

Tom Blake was older than Fox and Sam, younger than Frank and Johnny, somewhere in the middle, about three years older than Fox and me. Tom seemed at the time the most mature and the most serious of the lot. He provided a surrogate parental buffer between the hot-tempered Frank and the rowdy Johnny and the mischevious inclinations of Sam, Fox, and myself. Tom consistently declined the opportunity to take a drink of alcohol. He held firm against smoking and served in many respects, like Fox, as another Puritan in the family. Tom had in mind joining the U. S. Air Force when he finished high school. He had no money for college and saw the military as his ticket off Blake Hill and out of the poverty of Georgetown. Also, these were the years of the Vietnam War, and Tom must have known that, like Bob before him, he would likely be drafted into the infantry immediately after high school.

Fox possessed a combination of the best qualities of all his brothers. Refusing to smoke cigarettes with Sam and me when I managed a few times to sneak some of my father's Camels, Fox had the same moralistic traits as Tom. On the other hand, he loved having a good time. He relished the ball playing, dam building, crawfish cooking, snake hunting, rabbit trapping, and card playing that filled much of our leisure time. Our mutual love of playing ball of almost any sort made my father's onerous workdays even more burdensome for us. We viewed any sunny day as an opportunity for a good time at softball in the pasture or basketball on the hard-packed mud court we had made.

Fox seemed the most religiously inclined and attended church on a regular basis. Attending was easy, since the church was on the Blakes' property, only sixty feet from the back door of their house. Fox shared the good, rowdy fun of Johnny, possessed the strict conscience and moral restraint of Tom, held the rarely revealed, but obvious quiet sensitivity of Sam, and, if sufficiently provoked, could display rare flashes of Frank's temper. Fox's anger, however, was well controlled and always expressed verbally, rather than physically, and in an appropriate manner. His easy-going, steady nature in combination with Johnny's rocklike physique and quickness made physical fighting an option he was never called upon to use.

While the subject of race relations was only rarely brought up, I sensed that Fox was more aware than I of the emerging civil rights movement in the 1960s. Every now and then, he would make remarks about Reverend King from Atlanta and something called a protest march. These events seemed to me to be far away and not apt to affect life in Lincolnton one way or the other. As we became older teenagers in the late 1960s, Fox seemed to grow quieter and more serious, paralleling the chaos that was occurring in the outside world. I detected that his once-carefree demeanor changed significantly following President Kennedy's assassination. After that event, Fox seemed more serious. I could tell that he was often preoccupied with something. As a general rule, we avoided talking about unpleasant subjects.

We didn't know that our childhood friendship would come to be tested when ramifications of the civil rights movement wafted over Lincoln County in years to come. I would later think it curious that the subject of politics never entered our talks with each other. I believe we both feared that bringing up the topic of race would be an unwelcome intrusion into our friendship.

I remember only one instance when race became an issue on Blake Hill. It happened when we were playing ball with a gathering of Blake brothers and a number of black kids from Georgetown.

I had hit a line drive straight at the pitcher, Ronnie Johnson, who was about my age but smaller. I did not know Ronnie well, because he was not part of the regular card-playing crowd. The hard-driven ball had hit Ronnie directly in the face when he was unable to field it. For some reason, he took the accidental hit personally. His next pitch to me came like a bullet, aimed directly at my face. I turned aside to avoid the retaliatory strike but was nailed squarely on the back.

Seconds later, he charged at me, knocking me to the ground. As I rolled on the ground, doubled up in pain, I heard Ronnie call me a "cracker." Instantly, I went for his legs and pulled him down. Then we were on top of each other with fists flying. It was my first and only fight with one of the black kids from Georgetown. The fight, such as it was, ended in a minute or two with both of us unharmed and shoving each other angrily away.

The game came to a premature end as the group of ball players walked off the field. Ronnie seemed surprised that, instead of having the other black kids come to his aid, he was summarily derided as crazy and was inflicted with the ultimate moral condemnation of the Blakes when I heard Fox and Sam call him a fool. These were coded words of support for me and a clear message to Ronnie that messing with me and taking out his frustrations on their white buddy was not permissible.

I think the Blakes were ashamed that I had been the victim of a racial slur, the word "cracker" being reserved for only the most racist and malignant white characters, a word never used in public. Within a few days, however, we laughed about the fight and about how I had somehow "gotten Ronnie's goat." I never again heard the word "cracker." There was general consensus that I had "held my own" in the scuffle and that Ronnie had gotten out of line. Ronnie never apologized for the "cracker" remark, and after that episode, he rarely came to play ball on Blake Hill. When he did, he tended to ignore me. Ronnie seemed angry, but I was not sure whether the anger was related to me. I believe his generally sullen demeanor reflected some deeper source of resentment. He was hard to figure. Because of the unresolved tension that remained between us, I dreaded seeing him arrive.

Something ugly had entered our world that day, something that we all wanted to forget. I think the incident had frightened us more than the occasional surprise appearance of a water moccasin down at the creek.

So we have the cast of characters assembled on a fateful Sunday afternoon during my fifteenth year under an apple tree in the Blakes' backyard. This is how it happened, as the full story was related to me by the Blakes in the days that followed. My personal recollection of the events of that afternoon remains fuzzy. You will soon understand why.

The Blake brothers, Johnny, Frank, Tom, Sam, and Boyce, along with me and the three other visitors from down the path in Georgetown, Johnny Wayne Dorsey, Walter Sherrill, and Sylvester Cansler rounded out the number required for two simultaneous games. Ronnie Johnson had come and had left within minutes. I assumed it was because of me.

As the afternoon games progressed, Miss Ruth and Johnson Blake went to town. Shortly after their departure, Johnny produced a Mason jar that appeared to contain only purple grape juice. Addressing me, Johnny taunted with an air of great expectancy and pomp, "Zeke, I hear that you've been wanting to taste some 'shine. Now I know that you're a pitiful card player and don't have any real experience with women other than your mama, but I think it's about time we let you have a drink of liquor, that is, if you won't go and tell your mama about it." His comment was followed by one of his deep, rich, devilish laughs, while the older Blake brothers looked at each other in amusement. Each had something to say about the appropriateness of Johnny's offer of initiation into the world of manhood. Frank started first: "Go ahead and take a drink, Zeke. It won't kill you. Drinkin' is just like makin' love to a woman—not that you'd know much about that—but you got to start out slow and build up some experience. Me and Johnny talked this out, and we think it's about time you, Fox, and Sam started to learn a little somethin' about life."

Tom interrupted, "You two fools are going to get him drunk. Zeke never had any 'shine before, and how do you know it's not bad 'shine, anyway? How you gonna explain to his mama when you have to carry him home half-retarded and they have to put him back in the first grade?"

Tom then turned and lectured me, "Zeke, that stuff will make you sick, and Johnny and Frank ought to know you don't have any business drinkin' it, and that goes for Sam and Fox, too."

Predictably, Fox replied, "I sure ain't no fool. Johnny knows I don't want to drink, and if Miss Ruth finds out we been drinkin', we're all gonna have our butts torn up, and she'll go after Johnny's butt, too, even if he is married!" Laughter and debate went about in circles, and the card games proceeded. Treating their beverage with great respect, Johnny and Frank took careful sips of the Mason jar's mysterious, purple contents.

I had begged Johnny for years to get me some 'shine and let me see what it tasted like. Sam, age seventeen at the time, had been allowed to take a few sips, but the older Blake brothers strictly regulated any "sipping" by the younger ones. Evidently, sixteen was the age of initiation. I was delighted at the offer for a sip or two and considered the occasion practically the equivalent of taking my first Lutheran communion. I needed no convincing and ignored the warnings of Fox and Tom that I was going to get into trouble.

Without further debate, the jar was passed over to me. In a show of bravado, I took a large swallow and gulped it down in no time flat. "Hey, man. Go easy, fool," warned Johnny. "That's strong stuff."

"It tastes like watered-down grape juice to me!" I retorted boastfully. I was determined to show that I could hold my own and drink with the older brothers. I also wanted to prove to them, after years of unbearable teasing, that I was a "real man," like Johnny Blake.

"All right," broke in Johnny, "now you know what it tastes like. I hope you're satisfied, but you gotta be careful with that stuff because it'll hit you like a mule kicked you if you don't watch out. They don't call it white lightnin' for nothin', fool!"

Seizing the stage, I clutched tightly to the jar and refused to give it up. "All right, Johnny, you might be worried about my being able to hold my liquor, but you don't know much about that any more than you know about what I can do with a woman. I ain't gonna tell you about my women, but I can show you I can take a drink." With that, to Johnny's and everyone's visible horror, I began to "chug" the moonshine-and-grape-juice mixture. I had several gulps down before the no-longer-laughing, grim-faced Frank and Johnny made a collective lurch for the jar and my hand. It was as if they suddenly realized they had put a loaded pistol in the hands of a child and that child was putting the gun barrel into his mouth. When they tried to wrestle the jar back from me, it went flying across the table with the other card players dodging its toxic, purple spray. Together with my hand of cards, which I was still clutching, and my chair, I was knocked over to the ground.

"Damn you, Johnny Blake! First you try to get me to drink this stuff, and then you and Frank go and half kill me for doin' it. Now look what you done! How am I s'posed to explain my shirt and pants covered with grape juice to my mama?!"

The card games were completely disrupted. Whoever had managed to hold onto their cards had thrown them down on the table and were doubled up in fits of hysteria. Johnny Wayne Dorsey lay face down on the ground, beating his fists in the grass and howling. Sylvester Cansler, almost choking, was unable to speak during the height of the debacle. His head rested on the card table, from whence could be heard only intermittent bursts of cackling sounds. Johnny Wayne pulled himself together long enough to say to me, "All right, Zeke, you crazy fool, you give me your shirt and blue jeans, and I'll get my mama to wash them out for you! I'll tell her you got sick eating too many purple muscadine grapes."

While his comment was meant to be a joke, the alcohol was already taking effect on my brain. Again, to the horror of all, I began unbuttoning my shirt and pulling down my pants. I was soon standing before them dressed in only my underwear, my high-top tennis shoes, and white socks. I tossed my purple-soaked clothes over to a dumbfounded Johnny Wayne, who picked up and held the shirt and pants between his thumb and forefinger with arm outstretched as if my clothing were contaminated by cow manure.

Several of the Blake sisters heard the commotion from the house and peeped out the window. Bewildered to see me seminude and drunk and surrounded by the brothers they'd never seen in such an out-of-control state, they quickly closed the curtains. Shortly, Tom and Fox began to show signs of serious concern.

"Now look here, Johnny," I began, my voice becoming increasingly slurred, "I've put up with your jokes about the size of my 'you-know-what' for years. I just figure that if you'd really see what I got, then maybe you'd finally shut up!" Sensing what was about to happen, the card players began to scatter or otherwise cover their eyes. Johnny, meanwhile, lingered in a state of shock about the small, white teenage monster he had created. He stood frozen to the spot, wide-eyed, disbelieving, jaw dropped open. Before he could recover from his catatonic stupor, I turned around, dropped my Hanes briefs, and I shot Johnny "the moon." I muttered in a voice that had become almost incoherent, "Well, I ain't gonna show you the real thing 'cause I know you'd get jealous and probably depressed, and I don't want to hurt your feelings, Johnny. But I do want to thank you for the 'shine and give you the nice, white shine of my butt for you to remember me by!"

The exposure of my derriere was brief, but effective. Johnny and Frank, coconspirators in the afternoon's events, had stopped laughing. The mooning of Johnny Blake by anyone else in Georgetown, or even by one of the Blake family members themselves, would have resulted in something close to a death sentence delivered by Johnny's powerful jackhammer fists. Instead, Johnny, along with Frank, at last realized that they had a serious problem on their hand: What could they possibly do with this white boy, drunk on moonshine, without my mother finding out and without Miss Ruth skinning them alive, grown or not, married or not married, if she found out what had happened here under the family apple tree. But the outlandish scene was not quite over.

Sister Peggy emerged from the house and, with great effort to contain her amusement, she put on her best "Miss Ruth" impersonation of indignant rage and directed her shouting first at me. "Zeke Stoudemire," she addressed me with hands on hips, "I don't know what you think you're doing standing there almost buck naked in my yard, but you better get that white butt you seem to be so proud of out of here right now before one of the other girls sees you!" Immediately thinking of Punkin, even I was briefly jolted back to sobriety long enough to find my soggy pants and purple-stained shirt.

In fact, Punkin had toddled out the back door right behind Peggy without Peggy's notice. Rubbing her eyes, Punkin appeared to have just awakened from a nap. Not taking any chances, I pleaded with her not to tell Miss Ruth anything about our playing cards. I promised her I'd bring her a Moon Pie and some candy if she would not tell Miss Ruth anything she heard from her sisters. I hurriedly put the rest of my clothes back on before my knees gave way, and I keeled over in a stupor.

Peggy proceeded to blast the rest of the suddenly mute, guilty, older brothers, who shook their heads and stared at me on the ground, feigning disapproval. She began, "Well, I hope you smart-asses are satisfied. You've got one drunk, passed-out white boy on your hands. You better figure out a way to get him home before Miss Ruth gets here, and you sure got some explaining to do to Miz Stoudemire and his daddy!" With that pronouncement, she indignantly walked back to the house, all the while shaking her head back and forth and muttering, "Lord have mercy!" Once the door had slammed behind her, we could hear her loud release of pent-up laughter she'd barely managed to contain during her performance.

The Blake brothers aroused me as best they could and sat me up in case I vomited. I felt terrible. Johnny Wayne Dorsey, Sylvester Cansler, and Walter Sherrill had long fled down the dirt path toward home. They were not about to take part in the aftermath of this mess. After blame was traded back and forth for the situation Johnny and Frank had created, the group concluded that "it was Zeke's own damn fault," and a plan was made to get me home.

They would walk me or carry me down to the creek, wash my clothes clean in the creek as best they could, and keep me walking to try to sober me up a bit. When it became almost dark, they would sneak me up to the back door of my house while my parents were not looking and then direct me to my bedroom.

The plan went well. While supporting me on both sides and catching me when I stumbled or fell, they soon had me across their part of the pasture. Fortunately, I vomited when I got to the woods, which was a blessing, as it would help get the rest of the moonshine out of my stomach. At the creek, they splashed water on my clothes and scrubbed at the purple stains, which refused to budge, and cleaned off my face. I emerged from the water like one of the twice-born converts at a Sunday baptismal, yet stained and hardly sanctified.

Almost an hour had passed since my first drink of "purple Jesus." I was becoming vaguely aware of what it was like to be very drunk, and I kept thanking Fox, Tom, and Sam for trying to get me home. Frank and Johnny had remained behind to clean up the yard and to divert Miss Ruth's attention when she arrived home in hopes that she might not notice the absence of the other boys. She would be pleased to see all the older boys together again and to hear their promise to attend church with her the next morning.

Meanwhile, the three managed to propel me up the hill through the woods and, amazingly without tearing my clothes, over the last barbed-wire fence, the one that separated our yard from our cow pasture. Luckily, there was no sign of my parents outside, so they quickly shuffled me to the back door. They could see through the kitchen window as they passed it that my sister was watching television in the den. It would arouse suspicion if they came through the house holding me up, so they issued instructions on how to negotiate around the den to get to my bedroom. They told me to go to bed with my clothes on, and if my mother asked why I had gone to bed early, I was to tell her I had "gotten the flu," an excuse that would last well into the next day. They explained that the flu excuse would give me time to recover from my hangover and relieve me from going to church.

After opening the door for me, one of them gave me a shove, and my three escorts watched as I rounded the den en route to my bedroom and disappeared from sight. Then they sneaked around to my window to make sure I had made it into bed and had turned off the lights as they had further instructed. I had indeed followed orders and was soon asleep. The three Blake brothers were well on their way home when darkness fell. As I drifted back into consciousness, my head swimming, I could hear their rolls of laughter echoing through the woods.

The "flu" kept me home from school on Monday. My mother never suspected anything, although she found it odd that I had felt so bad that I had gone to bed in my clothes. On Sunday morning, I dragged myself out of bed and managed to get my shirt and pants into the washing machine in an effort to remove the last traces of purple stains.

Miss Ruth had arrived home about the time the younger Blake boys were disappearing into the woods. It was a narrow escape. The next day, the Blake brothers appeared together in church, a rare sight that may have provided an obvious sign of the collective guilt they shared, or perhaps their newfound piety was interpreted as an effort to cover up something or to exonerate themselves. If the church scene did not arouse her suspicion, the furtive laughter and whispering by varying groupings of her children, which Miss Ruth witnessed periodically throughout the day on Sunday, must have aroused her curiosity.

Mr. and Mrs. Blake had failed to notice that on Sunday, when I dragged myself out of bed to wash my clothes, I made my first bribe—a delivery of Moon Pies to Punkin to ensure her silence concerning my behavior that Saturday afternoon. She was kept well supplied with sweets for months to come.

Most of the rituals of my coming of age were shared in one way or another with the Blakes. We lived in a small world. It was as if nature had dissolved the cultural and social barriers that would have kept us apart in a city. In our world, we were equals, and we were brothers.

It was not long before my sixteenth birthday that I passed my next rite of passage. I fell in love with Mary Long from the mill village of Flat Shoals. As the courtship proceeded, aided by my newly acquired privilege—access to the family Sunday car, a relatively new, white, shiny Chevrolet four-door Impala, I learned little by little some things about her family. I uncovered a sad, painful side of her life, which explained what I had perceived as an unusual level of maturity, a seriousness about her, compared with that of most of the girls her age.

Mary had a younger brother who had been killed accidentally in a shooting accident while he was playing with some other boys when he was only twelve years old. Mary was almost sixteen when it happened. There remained some question as to the "accidental" nature of the tragedy, but I never knew and was reluctant to ask pointed questions about the details of his death.

I had learned, however, that on the night of the shooting, her twelve-year-old brother Michael had joined a group of his friends. Somehow, a gun had been brought out by one of them to "play with." A dark rumor circulated in the community that the boys had been playing a game of Russian roulette and that Michael was killed by a gunshot wound to the head.

Sharing with Mary physical features that distinguished the mother and daughter from the largely Scots-Irish folk of the mill village, Mary's mother also carried the same aura of sadness about her. The family's sadness was further compounded by the fact that her mother and father rarely spoke to each other. By Mary's report, the parents slept in separate bedrooms. Her father worked the late-night shift in the local mill. He had worked in the mill even as a young teenager, and the loud noise of the machinery had left him partially deaf. Mary lived in a home that had been visited by tragedy, about which neither of her parents ever seemed to speak. Hers was a family of unresolved and unspeakable grief.

In Flat Shoals, stories of hardship and tragic family events were not uncommon. Flat Shoals was a cotton mill village typical in its day, unique in its culture and sequestered from the rest of the world. It grew up around and derived its lifeblood from both the mill and the often turbulent, muddy South Fork River. The South Fork River and the cotton mill culture was as much a part of Lincoln County as farming and sank deep into the history of the place.

The lifeblood of the cotton mill villages was the South Fork branch of the Catawba River, which descended on the county from the northwest and meandered along the border of the town. The richest bottomland for farming originally lay along this river, and in time, the South Fork became the site of the cotton mills. The river created small valleys with banks that protected the mills and the inhabitants who built by the river, as long as one was wise enough to build above well-established high marks, where flooding historically had never occurred, even during the most torrential rains.

The river was unnavigable, except by canoes or small flat-bottom fishing boats. Unpredictably shallow in places, the river hid beneath its surface sharp rocks that could rip the bottom out of even the strongest boat hull when a vessel was carried over a run of rapids, which were common as the South Fork tumbled down to unite with the great Catawba.

The South Fork River ran along the fall line through Lincoln County from the higher mountainous regions of the Carolinas, where the land gradually broke down into the flatter terrain of the Piedmont to the east. Early pioneer mill builders like Diedrich Ramsour took advantage of the falling waters by harnessing its power as it cascaded down from the mountains to drive the wheels of the grinding stones that crushed into flour and various grades of meal the barley, wheat, oats, and corn of the local farmers.

The first cotton mill south of the Potomac River was built in 1816 at the McDaniel Spring, only a few miles east of the Lincoln County Courthouse, by two enterprising German immigrants, Michael Schenck and Absalom Warlick. As the South Fork of the Catawba River flowed through the county, this relatively narrow branch of the larger Catawba River was ideally located along the gentle descents in the elevation that created waterfalls. Where the river was narrow enough, dams could be built to turn paddle wheels, which then turned the machinery, and later, electric generators, for ginning and spinning cotton into thread and for weaving thread into cloth.

Soon cotton mills such as the one started by Michael Schenck and Absalom Warlick sprouted up and down the South Fork River. The mills took on names reflecting the characteristics of the sites on the river where they were built. Thus, there was the Long Shoals Mill and the High Shoals Mill. One established near the location of a Confederate medical laboratory that produced morphine from local poppies was called simply the Laboratory Mill. Another was the Massapoag Mill, the origin of which I never determined. Then there was the Wampum Mill. Wampum referred to strings of shells and beads used by the Indians as a form of money. The mill village that surrounded the mill was simply referred to as "The Wampum."

Hardworking, mostly Scots-Irish people who had originally migrated down from Virginia lived and worked in the mill villages on the South Fork River that ran through the town and county. The mill villages were isolated and provided a nearly encapsulated culture for their inhabitants. Mary had spent her entire life there. Her life in Flat Shoals was an altogether different one from that of the Blakes. In spite of their being worlds apart, however, Mary would one night unexpectedly meet the Blakes.

The mill villages, like Mary's Flat Shoals, were run in almost feudalistic fashion by the few wealthy families who owned the mills and the river land surrounding them. The residents of the villages often were derogatorily called "lint heads" due to the cotton lint that stuck stubbornly to their hair as they emerged from their shifts in the dusty, hot, and stuffy spinning and weaving rooms. Lint consisted of thick, fibrous, hairlike material that grew out of the cotton seed itself. It was not easy to remove once entangled in one's hair.

The former farm families who worked in the mills and lived in the villages that surrounded them had given up the unpredictability and hardship of eking out a living on the small farms they once owned in exchange for the meager but comparatively predictable paychecks from their work in the mills. They also benefited from the relatively cheap rents charged by the mill barons for the small wooden frame houses that were built at company expense around the mills for the workers to inhabit. An additional benefit for the employees was the generous line of credit extended to them at the mill's company stores until payday. Most of them considered themselves fortunate to have their mill jobs, and for some families, working in the mills became a multigenerational tradition.

When the former farmers gave up their land for the mill life, however, many lost their ties to the land. Subsequent generations of mill workers were relegated to the economically stable, but dreary, monotonous, mind-dulling life of the cotton mill. The originally quaint wood frame houses that surrounded the mills deteriorated over the years. By our time, some parts of these villages had become little more than white slums. Blacks were excluded from the mill villages just like they were excluded from most of the mill jobs.

With a very few exceptions, like Boyce's father Johnson, blacks were excluded from cotton mill jobs until the late 1960s. The few blacks who could land a mill job were generally given work the whites did not want, such as collecting trash or cleaning out the bathrooms, which historically were separate from toilets the blacks themselves might be allowed to use. In some cases, they were not allowed to use the mill's toilets at all.

The industrialist families who possessed the money and resourcefulness to build the original mills, like the Rhynes, Warlicks, Linebergers, Mauneys, Rhodes, Rudisills, and Schencks, were almost exclusively of German extraction. Some of these families soon found themselves barons of small fiefdoms, which consisted of the mill itself, a general store, and the surrounding frame mill houses rented to the workers. Ownership of the mills was private, usually with only one or two family investors. The ownership and operation were passed down in the family, along with the wealth accruing to these families, creating a small, emergent cotton-mill southern aristocracy.

Spinning raw cotton into spindles of yarn of varying thickness and quality, white men, women, and children operated these stuffy and poorly ventilated mills by working at least twelve-hour shifts six days a week. This routine kept the mills going twenty-four hours a day Monday through Saturday. Typically, workers "knocked off" at noon Saturday for the weekend break.

Every mill community had at least several churches, with each serving as the center of the community's social life. The churches were of three fundamentalist denominations: Baptist, Methodist, and varying types of charismatic Holiness or Pentecostal Churches of God. Since the small churches could scarcely afford to pay a man a full-time wage for his Wednesday night and Sunday services, most were part-time lay preachers who frequently held jobs in the mills and who claimed to have been called and seized by the Spirit to preach the Gospel. Women, of course, were prevented from being preachers according to the prohibitions of Saint Paul. Mary was a Baptist.

The small fundamentalist churches of the mill hills preached the Gospel of Jesus in its most literal form. Preachers would pound their fists on the pulpit threatening hellfire and brimstone unless one's sins were thoroughly washed clean in the blood of the Lamb. The pastors and parishioners spent a great deal of time pouring over and studying the Scriptures, but they seemed to have little understanding of how that enormously complex and ancient document came to be written and little understanding of the many meanings and mysteries it contained.

Life in the mill villages could be rough. There existed elements in the villages who sold illegal whiskey directly under the noses of the Baptist preachers, which, as predicted by the preachers, often led to violent, drunken fighting and disruption of marriages and families. One of the paradoxes of the mill villages was that all sorts of vices seemed to coexist almost naturally alongside the primitive piety and strict prohibitions of the church-saturated social culture. Notorious bullies who thrived on their reputations lived in each mill community, along with abusive, alcoholic, neglectful and wandering husbands.

Boys from the mill hill were reputed to enjoy ready access to illegal whiskey and to be prone to fight at the slightest provocation. The girls were considered as a rule more promiscuous than the more virtuous farm girls "from the country." The latter were raised, it was presumed, with more parental control and supervision and in areas where there were no dark streets or abandoned houses available for clandestine sexual rendezvous.

These presumptions, however, were based on unfair stereotypes. In truth, most of the people who lived in the southern mill villages were honest, hardworking, and seriously religious people. On the other hand, having lost their ties to nature and the land, they seemed to have lost part of their native spirit, as well, to the cotton dust of the mills.

I worked for one long summer in a mill by the South Fork owned by the Rhyne family. My primary job was unloading huge bales of cotton from trucks and storing them in the mill warehouse. I was lucky enough to be part of the "outside work crew" that consisted of three main characters who were tough, rough, strong men of the world named Hester, Stamey, and Elmore. I admired and liked them greatly. Our primary job was to unload the trucks, haul the mill's trash to the local dump, and take care of the routine maintenance of the mill and its grounds. We would also help with the maintenance of the Rhyne brothers' beautiful houses built on hills overlooking the mill itself. Being a member of the outside crew was an enviable assignment because it got you outside of the mill on a regular basis, and you enjoyed a variety of jobs, as well as some degree of freedom. Our shift started at 6:00 A.M. and lasted until 4:00 P.M. with a half-hour break for lunch and a few breaks in between. The Saturday work shift was from 6:00 A.M. to noon.

Because of the loud noise in the mill, many of the workers suffered headaches on a regular basis. A popular snack at break time would include an RC (for Royal Crown) Cola, spiked with a BC powder. Some workers drank Pepsi, Sun Drop, or Cheerwine, but RCs were generally preferred because they were thought to be higher in caffeine content and therefore better for headaches. The BC Powder was carefully poured from the small plastic packet in which it was sold. Originally, BC Powder consisted of aspirin, caffeine, and the potent analgesic phenacetin. When, over a period of years, a number of the mill workers developed kidney failure, it was discovered that prolonged use of phenacetin was the cause. The phenacetin was finally removed from the powder mixture, but the workers complained that BC Powders were never the same.

The combination of analgesic and caffeine from the BC Powder/RC gave the worker a little boost to get through the rest of the day. If you were hungry, another favorite snack during break time were "Vie-eeny sausages" (Vienna sausages). The little sausagelike pieces of ground meat from a variety of animal parts were packaged in small tin cans holding about eight two-inch "Vie-eenies." The meat of the sausage itself was often referred to as "mystery meat." The little sausages were best enjoyed by smearing them on saltine crackers and then chasing the "Vie-eeny" down the gullet, saltine and all, with a gulp of the RC and BC powder mixture. Dessert at break time or lunch often consisted of a Moon Pie, a local favorite.

"Break" was also time for a smoke, typically Winstons, which were thought to be the favorite cigarettes of the NASCAR racers, like Fireball Roberts and Richard Petty, all local heroes. The cigarettes only compounded the pulmonary condition called "white lung" or byssinosis, a fibrotic disease of the lungs caused by years of breathing the cotton dust of the old, poorly ventilated mills.

Fortunately, I could leave the mill for good at the end of the summer when school started again. Even though my high school girlfriend Mary Long would eventually leave her summer mill job at another village, I had a feeling that somehow the place would always stick to her just like the cotton stuck stubbornly to her raven black hair at the end of her shift.

I was perplexed by the contrast in appearance between Mary and the other girls in Flat Shoals until, upon further prodding about her family history, Mary revealed that one of her great-grandmothers on her mother's side of the family had been a Cherokee from the North Carolina mountains. The differences in her and her mother's appearance from the other women then became clear to me both in terms of their striking good looks and dignified, yet quietly sad, demeanor. They represented the last traces of Cherokee blood in the area.

The history of the Cherokee in that part of the world is another sad story. Mary formed a thin thread that linked me to it. Because of our discovery of arrowheads on the farm and what we believed were small burial mounds that I found with my brother and sister in the deeper sections of the woods, I was certain that Indians once lived in the area. Most of the Cherokee were removed from the Carolinas by President Van Buren in the winter of 1838 and herded by federal troops along the infamous Trail of Tears to the Oklahoma territory. Over a third of them died during the journey. Only a few successfully hid out in the mountains until the federal soldiers had left. At least one of these fugitives must have been Mary's ancestor. For unexpressed reasons, I had the impression that neither Mary nor her mother cared to find out her identity.

As high school proceeded, our relationship grew more serious. I scouted out places to "park" at night, places where we could make out with some degree of privacy after seeing a movie and getting a hamburger and milkshake at "It's." At It's, the locally famous drive-in restaurant, the short-skirted waitresses would sometimes serve you by gliding up to the car window on roller skates. It's was located at the end of the "cruising" loop on East Main Street, where, on Friday and Saturday nights, hundreds of teenagers made endless, aimless circles from one end of town to the other in their cars, U-turning around the courthouse square, where the circuit would start over again. You might park your car in front of one of the Main Street shops for a while, lean on the back of the car's trunk, and check out who else was cruising that night. If you were lucky, a carload of teenage girls might pull over to talk. If you were even luckier, one of them might join you for a ride. Mary and I had outgrown the cruising circuit and wanted a place to park in privacy.

In and around Georgetown and on my family farm, there were many country roads that were prospective sites for us. I was very pleased to find what I thought was the perfect place, familiar to nobody. Reaching the spot involved a short drive across an unused piece of pastureland where the fence was down.

Mary agreed to try out the place because it looked out-of-the-way enough to be safe from the sheriff's deputies, who seemed to take voyeuristic pleasure in catching young teenage couples in parked cars on lovers' lanes. A risk of such an isolated location was that of being discovered by rednecks like the Pratts, who might be out on a night of heavy drinking and who were known to take delight in terrifying and harassing young lovers, even blocking their cars, thus preventing them from leaving while they peeped through windows to see what was going on in the back seat.

While I never joined a raiding party with the Pratts, I was not altogether innocent of such prurient activities. On several occasions when we were in our early teens, Fox, Sam, and I camped out in the woods and hiked late at night to a favorite parking spot a mile or so from our campsite. The teenagers parked their cars at the end of a road banked by a small hill covered with trees. After letting the targeted couple settle in for a while and get warmed up with their amorous business, we would carefully position ourselves behind trees and bushes on the bank above the cars, and then, on a synchronized count, we would turn on our flashlights and spotlight the stunned and embarrassed pair. We hoped to catch a quick look at unbuttoned blouses and to see their startled, red faces. Then we would make a run for it while listening to the furious boyfriend's obscenities shouted out of the car window. We were lucky that they had not ever given chase.

These midnight flashlight ambushes ended the time we realized that we had flashed Johnny Farmer and his girlfriend Betsy Sharpe. We had committed what Johnny would consider a capital offense both against his privacy and the honor of his country princess, Betsy. We ran helter-skelter through the woods in fear for our lives. Johnny Farmer was out of his car within seconds, and had he not been slowed down by having to pull on some of his clothes, he surely would have caught one of us. After a brief chase through the woods, we scattered and hid. He gave up and stumbled back to his Mustang. Justice, however, awaited me.

I had completed my scouting for a place for Mary and me to park. Careful to avoid any spots beneath an embankment or hill, I decided on what I was convinced was the ideal site, secure from the probing eyes of the sheriff's deputies, adolescent sadists like the Pratts, and curious prepubescents as I myself had been.

It was a bright moonlit night, and though I turned off my parking lights so as not to attract any attention from any neighboring farmers, I easily found the place. I felt sure we were safe from the law, and my confidence that we were safe from the Pratts and their confederates increased when I noticed the lack of beer cans and any other signs of human interference in the area. What I had not counted on was that a recent rain had made the pasture wet. As I attempted to position the car to the side of the old dirt road, the car suddenly seemed to be sinking. With Mary close to my side, we were hopelessly stuck in the mud. I spun my tires forward and backward, but to no avail. By the time I stumbled out of the car, I was up to my ankles in mud, the car mired up to its axles.

It was already ten o'clock. Mary's curfew was eleven, and we were literally out in the middle of nowhere. It would take a wrecker to pull the car out of the mire, or so I thought. How would I ever get Mary home? How would I find a phone to call a wrecker? How would I pay for the wrecker? How would I explain to my parents and to hers what we were doing here, anyway? These overwhelming questions raced through my head, and every option seemed hopeless. We were in deep trouble, and Mary started to cry. My feet embedded in mud, I leaned against the car and tried to get my brain to work, to think what I could possibly do. Making our nightmare worse, car lights appeared to be moving slowly across the pasture. My heart began to race.

There was no blue light flashing, generally a common courtesy of the sheriff's deputies designed to alert lovers to fasten their buttons. We feared the worst. If it was the Pratts, or even worse, some drunk white trash I didn't know, I could be killed and Mary raped; things like that had happened before in Lincoln County. All I knew to do was to lock myself in the car with Mary and hope that whoever it was might pass by and leave us alone.

We slumped low on the floorboard in the front and

held our breath as the invading car inched closer, cautiously avoiding the mud that had gotten us in this fix. Our hearts continued to pound as the low rumble of the car with what sounded like noisy double-barrel carburetors and twin mufflers grew louder, and as it pulled up directly alongside us. Then there followed an abrupt silence and ominous darkness. The motor and lights had been turned off. The silence seemed endless. Then we heard several car doors open and slam, but no voices. Mary squeezed my hand. Knowing there was absolutely nothing we could do, and expecting the worst, we simply froze.

After what seemed an interminable length of time, I opened my eyes and looked upward from my position on the floor toward the passenger window. What I saw was a frightening face squarely plastered against the window such that its appearance was distorted and bizarre. Then the face moved back from the glass a bit and evolved into an eerie grin replete with a set of gleaming white teeth that glowed in the darkness, and next, from it came a burst of laughter, joined by a growing chorus of laughter from a group whose faces had now appeared at every window of our car.

"Well, well, well, if it ain't ol' Zeke out gettin' some for himself! Why, I bet he's glad we showed up, so we could tell him where to find it!"

Like a black angel from heaven, it was none other than my bid whiz partner and moonshine mentor Johnny Blake.

After reassuring an embarrassed Mary that "Hey, I know these guys," I was out of the car being greeted with smiles and slaps on the back from Johnny, Frank, Sam and Johnny Wayne Dorsey, all of whom had "had a few" and who seemed to grasp with delight the desperate nature of my situation. They couldn't stop laughing long enough to hear my pleas to help me get a wrecker and to loan me some money to pay for it.

When Johnny finally collected himself, he said to me, as he milked the moment for all he could get out of it, "Well, ol' Zeke, I guess that little moonshine episode got you off to a good start. I can't tell you how proud I am of you! But let me tell you something, Zeke. Next time you bring some girl out here to the woods trying to get you some you-know-what, try to stay out of the mud, boy! There's other things you'd probably rather get stuck in, if you know what I mean!" This comment sent them into another round of howling laughter, slapping of knees, and stomping about the moon-swept pasture, unable to contain their enjoyment of my hapless situation. Soon after that, without a word, while Mary waited speechlessly, embarrassed and confused about what was going on outside the car, Johnny ordered me back into the car, and the Blake brothers and Johnny Wayne gathered around.

"Now start it up, Zeke, you damn fool, and put it in reverse. Try to back it out of here real slow-like without killing us." Doing as I was told, the wheels began to spin, and as if by magic, we were suddenly back on hard ground. Sam, being the youngest, had been placed in the back of the car, the most hazardous position for "the lift." As he scrambled to safety, he fell, rolled onto the pasture grass, and resumed his cacophony of laughter. The brothers had literally lifted the car with both Mary and me inside it onto firm, dry pastureland with their strong shoulders, just as they once lifted me out of my childhood loneliness and isolation years before.

Johnny walked around to the driver's side of the car where I sat. I stuck out my hand to him. "Thank you, man, but you about scared us to death when you first showed up. How'd you know about this place, anyway?"

Mary was now feeling safe. Seeing Johnny's friendly, smiling face, she thanked him, too. "Well, Zeke, you got to remember that I been ridin' these hills a lot longer than you, and I know all the good places to hide with your liquor or your women if you want some privacy. Now since they won't let the black folks in the drive-in movies, I know all kinds of places like this, but boy, I'd suggest that you stick to the drive-in until you can tell mud from dry road. And for God's sake, boy, don't go drinkin' any more 'shine unless I'm there to look after you! I hope Mary over there can keep you out of trouble. Somebody sure as hell needs to!"

I thought that he was finished with me, but I was not so lucky. After reflecting a moment, he continued in all seriousness, "Oh yeah, I got one other idea. I'll tell Johnny Farmer you're having trouble finding a place to park. I'm sure he'd like to help you out. Yeah, old Johnny Farmer, I know he'd want to know all about your troubles out here on Lovers' Lane!"

I realized he must have found out from Sam and Boyce that I had been a part of the raiding party that had "flashed" Johnny Farmer and Betsy Sharpe years before, an unsolved crime that had become legendary in Georgetown and along Victory Grove Church Road. Johnny Farmer was still trying to find the perpetrators. I knew Johnny Blake was only joking. I could trust Johnny Blake not to rat on me. Besides, after all these years, we had enough information to blackmail each other for eternity.

Johnny joined his brothers and Johnny Wayne in his car, and they followed me until I was safely out on the main road and heading toward Mary's home in Flat Shoals. Greatly relieved, I pulled into her driveway at precisely 10:55 P.M. and said a silent prayer thanking God for my good friend Johnny Blake and the rest of the black angels from Georgetown.

The Only White Boy We Trusted

> We are all brothers to all who have trod
> the earth; brothers and heirs to dust and
> shade: maybe to immortality.
>
> —Elbert Hubbard

During most of our boyhood, Fox and I were unaware that a social revolution was soon to break out in the South over integration and across the country over America's involvement in Vietnam. The Kennedy assassination in 1963 seemed to affect Fox deeply. Until we were about to graduate from high school, however, we remained relatively sheltered from the growing turmoil that was stirring in distant places.

The Supreme Court ruled in 1954 that separate but equal schools were unconstitutional, but it was another fourteen years before the schools in Lincoln County were finally forced by the federal government to fully integrate. This was very good news, as far I was concerned. I would be able to hang around and play ball every day on the same school athletic teams with Fox and the rest of my Georgetown friends, as well as with their black friends who lived in town, most of whom I had come to know pretty well. The fun, peace and quiet that Fox and I enjoyed as boys was not to continue forever; our halcyon days of relative innocence were about to come to an end.

The first year of forced integration was to start in the fall of 1968, just as Fox and I were entering our senior year of high school. By then, Sam and Tom had already completed their years at Newbold, the all-black high school that was being converted to an elementary school. Tom had joined the air force and would shortly be sent to Vietnam. Sam was waiting to see what would happen and hoping he could avoid the war altogether. For those of us still in high school, we believed President Johnson when he told us that it would not be long before the fighting was over. We felt we had little to worry about.

Among my other friends, Paul Lawing seemed the most preoccupied with Vietnam, because his brother-in-law, with whom he was very close, had been killed there. Paul had vowed to join the army after he finished high school and seemed intent on going to Vietnam to avenge his brother-in-law's death. The other rumor about Paul claimed that he was angry and depressed over losing the love of his life to another friend of mine and that he planned to join the army out of bitterness and spite.

With the war looming in the background, plans for the federally mandated integration of our high schools began in the spring of 1968. Few black or white students shared my enthusiasm at the prospect. The blacks were proud of the tradition at their own Newbold High and resented being shipped to a strange new high school where they would be the minority. In fact, the black students would represent little more than ten percent of the entire student body at Lincolnton High School (LHS). The black students were losing the teachers and coaches whom they admired and trusted, and who had served as valuable role models for them.

The majority of students at Lincolnton High were from our small town of about five thousand people, and the rest of the high-school-age students attended all-white county high schools. Given the fact that few blacks had ever been allowed to buy enough land to farm in the county, there were relatively few black families living outside a four- or five-mile radius of town. The student body of Lincolnton High School at that time consisted of only about eight hundred white students. Approximately one hundred black students were to be transferred from Newbold High.

In an effort to pacify the federal officials overseeing integration efforts in the South, for a few years prior to

1968, the school board initially offered a "freedom of choice" arrangement, which meant that students could go to any county school they wished within their district, black or white. Newbold, the only black high school in the entire county, was located a few miles from the town square on the outskirts of town. The black students from the far western and eastern parts of the county would have to ride over twenty miles by bus and often pass right by white high schools in order to reach Newbold. To make an eight o'clock class at Newbold, many were picked up as early as 6:00 A.M.

Even so, only a few black students drifted over to Lincolnton High School from 1966 through 1968, and no white students chose to attend Newbold. By 1968, there were only five or six black students at Lincolnton High, their number dwarfed by the student body of over seven hundred whites. The black students had little desire to come to Lincolnton, officially named for Stephen Dodson Ramseur, the famous young general in the Confederate army and a local icon of those who in one way or the other were still loyal to the Confederate cause.

Many of the blacks feared they would be shunned and targeted for discrimination at the white high school. Tension over the integration of the schools was building in both the black and white communities, as well as fear that even violence at school might be the result, common in other parts of the South during those days. An entire era in America was coming to an end, and Boyce and I suddenly found ourselves on the edge of great change.

In 1968, Mary and I were still dating. In fact, we were "going steady," and we were both anxious about what would happen to our relationship when we went off to college. There was a serious question as to whether Mary was going to college at all. Her father didn't really think it was necessary, as she could get a good job in the cotton mill until she got married, even if she didn't happen to marry me. He was not willing, or was not able, to help her financially to go to college. It was my guess he wanted her to stay at home after high school and had, with regard to her education, no greater hopes for or expectations of her. Probably suspecting I would be out of the picture soon enough, he generally ignored me.

I loved Mary very much, and I hoped there would be some way for her to get out of the mill village, not just because I wanted to be close to her at college, but because Mary was too intelligent and refined in her own way to remain trapped in Flat Shoals only to pick cotton lint out of her head at the end of the day. If she were limited by her father's ambitions for her, she was likely to become a mother before the age of twenty, married to one of the local mill workers. We planned together how she could raise enough money from her summer mill job and through scholarships to attend the state university where I was heading.

Boyce, the name Fox preferred to be called at school, had expressed college hopes. His best chance, he figured, was at the local community college. He could earn enough by working in the mills to pay its small tuition. At the end of the 1960s, the cotton, textile, and furniture mill jobs were just being opened to blacks, although Boyce's father, Johnson, had been working at the Mauney-owned Long Shoals cotton mill for thirty years by now.

As the 1960s progressed, I became increasingly aware of the many discriminatory practices of our country, which I had never noticed before. I could see that things that seemed at one time so natural to me were terribly abnormal. Like most other Southerners of the day, I had unconsciously regarded segregation as simply a way of life, the way things just were.

Listening to the speeches of John Kennedy and to those of Martin Luther King Jr. brought about a gradual awakening for me, as it did for so many others in America, to the fact that I was living in a racist society. In many respects, the blacks in the South were not much better off than they had been after Reconstruction. The KKK remained active in many parts of the South. It was no secret that Lincoln County was home to a number of Klan members.

The Vietnam War heated up by the mid-1960s, and many of my classmates desperately sought ways to avoid being drafted. You could get a deferment if you were in college or medical school, or if you could manage to be assigned to the North Carolina National Guard. Some worked through political connections to do so. Serving military duty in the Guard would at least keep you out of the jungles of Vietnam. This means of escape from Vietnam, however, was not open to blacks, as they were all but completely excluded from joining the N.C. National Guard.

Storm clouds were gathering not just over North Carolina, but over all of the United States. As the civil rights movement gained steam, troops from North Vietnam and arms from the Soviet Union and Communist China poured into Southeast Asia and ended President Johnson's naive hopes for a brief war. It began to dawn on Americans that with ostensibly good intentions to defend freedom and democracy and to rid Vietnam of communism, we had been drawn into a war we could not win.

My once-bucolic little county began to send its young men off to war in a place that many people still had trouble finding on a map. During my sophomore year, Ralph Smith, the only son of one of my high school English teachers, Mrs. T. E. Smith, had been shot down and killed in his helicopter in South Vietnam. His mother's grief was painfully obvious to us on a daily basis.

My high school football coach's only son was a marine in Vietnam. Every day at practice, we could read the worry on his face. Several of the older boys I played football with, like Doyle Brinson and Terry Hager, had been wounded in combat. Spencer Sigmon, one of my older friends, had been blown up by a land mine and killed instantly. Frank Cauthen, a regular pasture-ball teammate, had been killed. As we approached our senior year, our high school class understood that the war would not end anytime soon. We would not escape facing this far-off war. It was a long way from Lincolnton to Saigon, but the distance seemed to be growing shorter and shorter.

Martin Luther King Jr. was assassinated in April 1968, and soon thereafter, the local school board received a federal order to fully integrate the county schools. It was during this turbulent time in America that Boyce and his friends stepped off the school bus at Lincolnton High on the first day of school, August 1968.

My father had taken me to school early that first day. I wanted to be there when Boyce arrived. The white students milled about the schoolyard, and a quiet, but noticeable tension and air of expectation pervaded the waiting white crowd. Several buses pulled up to the curb, emptied its white students, and left. The first bus of black students had yet to arrive. It should come soon. No one knew what to expect.

Finally, the first bus with black students could be seen pulling into the school driveway. From the few faces I glimpsed as it passed by me before it came to a stop in front of the school, I felt sure it brought kids from the Georgetown area. I could not see Boyce. When the bus came to a halt, the door opened, and the first noticeably anxious, somewhat disoriented black students slowly descended the steps of the bus. They cautiously looked about them and made their first contact with their new school grounds. A large group of white students gathered around the bus. I didn't hear a word. The blacks were greeted initially with a hostile silence. Reactions from the white students ranged from indifference, dismissiveness, and curiosity to silent resentment. Standing a ways back in the group, I began to hear a few barely audible slurs. Several of Lincolnton High's leading bullies had taken it upon themselves to get positioned at the front of the crowd in order to present a threatening presence.

The black students clustered awkwardly and insecurely at the curb beside the bus, unsure of what to do or where to go. They remained fixed in place, talking quietly among themselves. Finally, I saw Boyce walking down the steps of the bus. He seemed to be searching the white bunch before him. I knew he must be looking for me. I broke the uncomfortable quiet.

"Fox!! Fox!! Hey, Fox!! Over here, man!" I shouted to him and began making my way to the front. Although I would be no match in a fistfight with some of the school toughs who stood at the front and who might be intent on starting trouble, I was, nevertheless, co-captain of the football team that senior year and garnered a little respect from them by virtue of that position. Members of the football team stuck together, and as I negotiated toward the bus, I spotted my backup, who were now following behind me. There were the big guards and tackles Terry Reinhardt, Mike Cline, Colin Rudisill, and Larry Yoder. My best white friend, co-captain of the team, quarterback, future West Pointer and eventual trauma surgeon Scott Norwood showed up, and Kim Rudisill, Scott's backup quarterback and another of my best friends, had materialized as well. They had already become acquainted with Boyce since football practice had started several weeks before classes and the official beginning of the school year.

When I reached Fox, he greeted me with a warm, relieved grin. His first words were, "Zeke! Where you been, man?! I been looking all over for you!"

"I've been looking for you, too. What did you do, sit on the back of the bus? Don't you know that black folks don't have to do that anymore?" I laughed, but Boyce's response was delayed. It took a few moments for him to get my joke.

"Oh, man, now don't get started with me! I should have known you'd come up with somethin'! Now, what in the heck are we supposed to do?"

The other black students bunched up around us, and I began to recognize more familiar faces. While we shook hands with each other, several of my white friends, in addition to the members of the football team, began to appear one by one. The color-divided crowd of students became an increasing mix of both colors as Boyce and I were busy introducing white and black students to each other. The tension was broken, at least for a while.

Noticing the time, I said to Boyce, "You guys, come on with us. We'll show you where to go." So Boyce and I led this first group of black students up the steps of Lincolnton High School. Several of my white friends trailed behind chatting with other black students, who still were obviously wary and uncomfortable. The first day of school had begun.

The first tense days of classes passed. Whenever I saw black students from Georgetown, they appeared particularly glad to see me, and the feeling was mutual. I had looked forward to the day when the fun we had out in the country could be transferred to the daily grind of school life. Most of the black students from the area were familiar with the friendship between Fox and me. I think many of the black kids felt reassured by the sight of a familiar face amidst a sea of strange white faces. As Boyce put it to me in later years, while we were recalling those first days of integration, "You were the only white boy we trusted!" I took that as a great compliment.

Justifiably anxious, the black students had little idea of what would be expected of them academically or socially in the new environment into which they had been thrust. In spite of the fact that Newbold High had well over thirty black teachers, only one was transferred to Lincolnton High, and none of their athletic coaches were transferred.

Boyce had already been given entree to the football team and introductions to the coaches. I told them I had been playing ball with Boyce for years and that he was "really fast." My easy familiarity with all of the blacks who were trying out for the team had helped make integration of the football team go well. Also, the coaches had eagerly awaited the influx of fresh, new talent. With the infusion of the best members of the Newbold team, there was every chance we might take the state championship for the first time that year.

During the first few weeks of school, there was no overt violence between blacks and whites, only a feeling of general mistrust. The other white students must have noticed me as I moved about easily with the black students, and it must have been obvious that we genuinely liked one another. I had developed through my relationship with the six Blake sisters a special knack for teasing and joking with the black girls, as well.

There was, however, no question at the time that strict, unspoken social boundaries around the issue of interracial dating were to be observed. The idea of interracial dating was probably inconceivable to anyone. Most of the black girls already had boyfriends and their own social network, and vice versa for the white students.

Things seemed to be moving along smoothly, especially among the boys because of the easy integration of the football team. The black and white girls, on the other hand, kept their distance from each other. Unlike the boys, who participated together on sports teams, the girls had very little in common and few opportunities to really become acquainted. At the start of that first year of integration, the black and white girls were not yet playing sports together. The only female athletic team was basketball, anyway. The distance between the girls was there from the first day and seemed to widen as the year progressed.

Most of the school clubs were established during the prior school year and were, of course, all white. No concerted effort was made to invite the black students to join. So many things could have been done and should have been done to make them feel welcome and part of the school. All of us, however, were on unfamiliar ground as to how to proceed with this new social phenomenon. None of us had any experience.

The school council officers for Lincolnton High had been elected the previous year and were, of course, white. Along with my athletic position, my role as vice-president of the student body gave me some political visibility to help the process of integration, which not only felt natural to me, but fun. At first, my closeness to the black students and to Boyce must have seemed curious to the whites. Boyce and I were always together. We ate together and joked together. In fact, because of him, my nickname "Zeke" caught on with all my white friends, too. It was plain to see that we enjoyed each other's company immensely.

We also formed a pair of sorts on the football team, where I played defensive halfback. Boyce was my counterpart and played offensive halfback. Only after I was older did I appreciate the historical coincidence represented by the fact that the football field where we practiced and played was located on the exact site of the Battle of Ramsour's Mill. There, near the South Fork River, where the defeated Tories had beaten their hasty retreat, the Patriot collaborators Fesso and Adam Reep had celebrated their joyful reunion on June 20, 1780, almost two hundred years before.

While the first year of forced integration was launched smoothly enough, trouble came from an unexpected source. Whereas the football team was integrated with ease, the selection of cheerleaders was a different story. The choice of cheerleaders was made by a small group of teachers who evaluated the tryouts. The grooming of the cheerleaders at LHS generally started in junior high. The younger girls would curry favor with the more senior cheerleaders, who helped them learn and practice the cheers and the various gymnastic routines involved. Some degree of politicking occurred, with ambitious cheerleader candidates going out of their way to "suck up" to the teachers known to be on the selection committee. Becoming a cheerleader ensured celebrity social status, instant popularity, and dating success. The position of cheerleader was more prestigious and sought after than any academic award the school offered.

In early September, black girls who had been cheerleaders at their former schools and other black girls with cheerleading aspirations arrived at the tryouts. They did not know the standard cheers or routines of the white girls, and when it was all over, Lincolnton High School had, as before, an all-white varsity cheerleading squad.

The resentment among the black students should have been anticipated, and moreover, it should have been prevented. The black girls were angry and humiliated. Word that they had been discriminated against in the selection process spread to their boyfriends and around the black community. The all-white selection committee of female teachers insisted that the process was "perfectly fair," that it was simply a matter of the black girls' lack of familiarity with the traditional LHS cheers and the accompanying drills and gymnastics required. They just needed a year or two to "catch up."

Tension grew between black and white students. The discrimination perceived in the cheerleading selection confirmed what many of the blacks had expected and predicted all along, that they were going to be left out at Lincolnton High School, that the white kids would dominate every aspect of school life, that they would be second-class citizens, at best. The cheerleading selection debacle became emblematic of the discrimination they had anticipated at Lincolnton High.

Matters were made worse at the time of elections for class officers for the year. Several black students were nominated for office, but all were defeated. Gossip spread quickly that the voting had been rigged against them, since the job of counting the ballots had been delegated to an all-white group of students loosely supervised by white teachers. The black students, especially the black girls, already inflamed by the cheerleading issue, demanded a recount. Anger in the school mounted. One could almost smell a burning fuse that was bound to lead to an explosion of resentment and possibly violence.

The flash point of ugly trouble began when "Tanker" Sherrill, a big-mouth redneck, made this comment one day in the schoolyard loud enough for all to hear: "Those niggers had their own school and should go back to it and take all their Watusi women with them." I was standing nearby and winced when I heard him. I hoped that none of the black students had heard his foolish words or at least that those who did would choose to ignore him, as most of the white kids had learned to do over the years. But it was not to be a good day for Tanker. His mistake was making his insults within hearing distance of a certain Mary Jane Diamond.

Mary Jane had earned a reputation for being both one of the most likable, yet toughest, of the black girls. There was talk she carried a knife in her purse for protection, particularly if she were hassled by the likes of a Tanker Sherrill. She was also the sister of Sylvester Diamond, one of my best buddies and all-time favorites. Sylvester was an affable, funny guy, who was also the stocky, muscular, fast, agile, rock-solid fullback on our football team that year.

Sylvester had the reputation of one who was not prone to fight because he was never actually challenged to fight. "Any fool," as Boyce would say, "would be dead on arrival with no chance of survival" if they were to catch a fist-to-jaw from the incredibly strong tank that was Sylvester Diamond. I thought of Sylvester as the equivalent of a nuclear bomb; he didn't have to use his fighting potential because everyone knew that if he got angry about anything, there was bound to be mass destruction of someone's face.

Sylvester was really a gentle person at heart and was well respected, not just for his friendliness and athletic skills, but for the quiet way he controlled his innate power. His sister Mary Jane possessed the good-natured friendliness of her brother Sylvester, but in contrast to him, she was not known for containing her anger when provoked. Mary Jane could be volatile. Even her brother seemed to keep his distance from her when she was in a bad mood.

Mary Jane overheard Tanker Sherrill's comments in the schoolyard during that fateful lunch break, as I and most of the other students milled about in mostly segregated clumps. The leading topic of discussion among students that day was the question as to whether or not there would be "trouble over the cheerleader thing" and the black students' demands for a recount of the vote for class officers, since only whites had been elected. The mood in the school was especially tense, since fast approaching was the first football game of the season, where the sharp contrast between the integrated football team and the all-white cheerleading squad would be paraded before the entire town and student body.

Having overheard Tanker's words, which he took no discretion in muting, I saw Mary Jane stop talking and appear to think for a moment. Then she slowly, but menacingly, unzipped her purse, while walking over to the group of white boys that included Tanker. When the other white boys saw her heading their way and her hand moving into her purse, they must have concluded that Tanker had gone too far. His companions stepped back, way back. As I observed this event unfold from a different vantage point, I suspected that indeed Tanker's voice was likely to undergo a surgically induced change to a higher pitch, that is, if he were lucky enough to have a voice at all after Mary Jane was through with him.

Tanker defiantly squared off to face Mary Jane, who moved closer to him, zeroing in on her target. Students, black and white, began to circle them, but gave them a very wide berth. It was high noon in the schoolyard. The crowd stood still and quiet. "What did I hear you say, Tanker Sherrill? Did I hear you say something about us black folk should go back to Newbold High School, and did you say something about some niggers? Is that what you said, white boy?" taunted Mary Jane, hand on her hip and the other one in her purse, eyes squinting as she glared at him.

When Tanker's buddies cleared away from him, Tanker must have known he was in trouble. He would have to face Mary Jane Diamond alone. Even the most redneck white student was embarrassed by Tanker Sherrill. No one was about to defend his loud, obnoxious, and filthy mouth. On the other hand, Tanker knew that to back down in front of all the white and black students would mean unbearable humiliation. Instead, he puffed up with even more bravado.

"Naw, Mary Jane, I didn't say you jungle bunnies ought to go back to Newbold. I said you ought to go back to Africa and swing in the trees and eat bananas with the rest of your relatives!"

Before Tanker could react and reach for his own knife, Mary Jane had pulled a large straight razor from her purse and was headed in a charge for Tanker. The girls in the crowd screamed. The guys stood transfixed by what we thought was going to be a real live murder taking place right before our eyes. No one made a move to help Tanker. He was clearly on his own this time.

Tanker turned and ran for his life. He must have quickly figured that his best bet was to get to safety in the school building for that was the direction in which he was headed. There he could find a teacher to protect him. He knew Mary Jane would not hurt a teacher. What Tanker did not know was that, alerted by another student more attentive to what was going on outside that day than in what his teacher was saying, Mary Jane's brother Sylvester had watched the better part of the scene from the window of an upper-level classroom and figured that Tanker had said or done something pretty bad to enrage Mary Jane to the point of drawing her razor blade on him. Sylvester must have realized that Tanker's manhood, if not his life, was in imminent jeopardy.

Sylvester had no special love for Tanker. Like most of the white students, he viewed him as despicable but generally ignored him whenever possible. He was a fool unworthy of challenging.

Apparently, Sylvester saw that Mary Jane was about to lose it, immediately left his classroom without a word, and moved quickly down the steps closest to the target door of Tanker's run for safety. Mary Jane ran behind him in hot pursuit. All eyes were transfixed on the chase. Then Tanker looked ahead and saw in terror that blocking his entrance to the school stood a grim-faced Sylvester, waiting for him, arms quietly folded, his head shaking slowly back and forth. I followed the drama from a distance, jogging way behind

Mary Jane. She wouldn't hurt me, but I planned to take no chances. I had no intention of ending up in the middle of the fray between Tanker and Mary Jane.

Tanker must have been convinced beyond any doubt that he was about to die. He turned around briefly only to see Mary Jane's razor flashing in the sunlight not far behind him. Sylvester was sternly planted in front of him. He gave one last backward glance at Mary Jane, then turned and found himself facing her brother. With tears in his eyes, he pleaded, "Sylvester! Sylvester! Don't let her kill me! Please, Sylvester, please!"

A split second before Mary Jane would have been upon him, Sylvester pulled back his mighty right fist and slammed it squarely into Tanker's left jaw, dropping him like a rock to the ground, where he curled up moaning in a semiconscious fetal position. Turning to his enraged sister, who was standing above the incapacitated Tanker with razor still drawn, Sylvester tried to calm her down. "All right, Mary Jane," he lectured, "I don't know what this fool said to you, but it ain't worth your getting into any trouble about it. Now put that razor away and get out of here." Mary Jane seemed satisfied to see Tanker flattened, and she generally listened to her brother, as he had a cooler head than she.

Mary Jane's razor disappeared. As she was walking away, she noticed me standing a safe distance away. Glancing at me, she quipped, "Well, Zeke, did you get your eyes full?" She did not stop for me to respond, as if there was anything I could say. She marched away.

When Tanker gradually came about and found his wits, Sylvester helped pull him up. "Come on, fool, let me get you to the bathroom to get you cleaned up." Lecturing Tanker on the art of survival, he said, "Don't you know any better than to mess with Mary Jane? Hell, man, I don't even mess with Mary Jane, and I'm her brother!"

Tanker, contrite and humbled, responded, "Thank you, Sylvester. You saved my life. Tell Mary Jane that I'm sorry and that I didn't really mean anything by what I said. I was just runnin' my mouth off."

"You'll have to tell her you're sorry yourself, you damn fool! Otherwise, you better watch your backside. I can't be here to save your sorry butt all the time," Sylvester advised. "I'll try to keep her from hurting you in the meantime, but you better make it up good with her. I sure as hell wouldn't want Mary Jane on my tail! You better watch yourself, Tanker."

Sylvester led Tanker by the arm into the nearest bathroom. The bell indicating the end of lunch rang. Like a slightly disgruntled bear, Sylvester ambled on to his next class, silently passing me as he shook his head back and forth. Tanker was left to collect himself as best he could. I assumed he must be thinking how he could accomplish the seemingly impossible tasks of making peace with Mary Jane

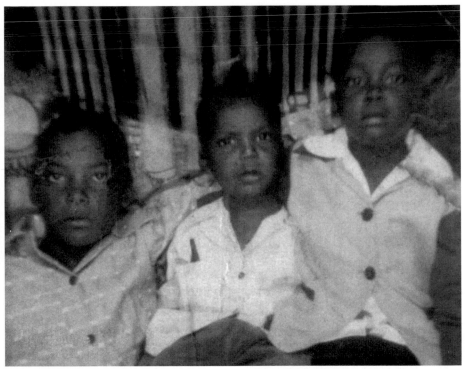

FRANK, SAM, AND TOM BLAKE

JOHNNY BLAKE (1941-1991)

SHIRLEY BLAKE IN 1942

FUTURE SHERIFF BARBARA PICKENS WITH HER FIRST PATROL VEHICLE

SHERIFF HARVIN CROUSE

GRAVE OF CONFEDERATE GENERAL
STEPHEN D. RAMSEUR (1837-1864)

JOHNNY WAYNE
DORSEY

SYLVESTER CANSLER
(1949-1996)

WALTER SHERRILL

SAM BLAKE

TOM BLAKE

FRANK CAUTHEN

ABANDONED LONG SHOALS COTTON MILL

Cotton mill village church

This is It (It's)

The 1968 Senior football players: 1st row: Steve Hipp, Ricky Helms, Kim Rudisill, Johnny Colvard. 2nd row: Randy Saunders, Scottie Norwood, Colin Rudisill, Terry Reinhardt, Alan Stoudemire. 3rd row: Boyce Blake, David Frye, Richard Goodin, Larry Hubbard, Mike Cline. 4th row: Bobby Joe Easter, Sylvester Diamond, Sylvester Cansler. (Larry Hunter and Maurice Moore are not pictured.)

BOYCE BLAKE   ALAN STOUDEMIRE

THE 1968 LINCOLNTON HIGH SCHOOL CHEERLEADERS: 1ST ROW: KAY
CARPENTER, CINDY CARTER, JUNE BROOME, DEBBIE LATTIMORE, JILL
SENTER. 2ND ROW: BECKY BURRIS, CAROLE COCHRANE, SANDI ROBINSON,
AND MASCOT, JANIE ADERHOLDT.

SAM ROBINSON
(1951-1969)

KAY CARPENTER

KIM RUDISILL

SHIRLEY BESS

BEVERLY SIMMONS

CHYRAL REINHARDT

NELSON WALLACE

STEVE SUTTLE

SYLVESTER DIAMOND
(1950-1974)

SCOTTIE NORWOOD

B. J. BLAKE, BOYCE'S SON (AGE 7)

BOYCE C. BLAKE WITH B.J.

and, at the same time, saving face with his peers after the day's humiliation.

There was likely to be more trouble to come in spite of Sylvester's promise to try to keep Mary Jane under control. Both white and black students considered that justice had been well served by Mary Jane and Sylvester Diamond that day. On the other hand, rumors fanned out around town that violence had broken out at the school. In fact, in the ensuing days, several windows and lights were broken by unidentified parties, and a fire had been started in one of the school bathrooms. The result was an evacuation and an exaggerated response by the fire department to extinguish what turned out to be flaming toilet tissue inside a trash can. Word had it that the fire was related to the animosity that still festered and grew regarding the exclusion of black girls from the cheerleading squad. There was even whispering that "the school will burn next."

Verbal taunts escalated between black and white students. Some shoving in the halls occurred, too, but most of the problems consisted of verbal hostility and mumbled slurs. The mounting tide of resentment showed no signs of subsiding.

When the local newspaper printed an article on the growing "racial unrest" at the high school, both white and black parents began pulling their children out of school. The daily census dropped by almost fifty percent.

The once bustling halls now seemed eerily empty and abnormally quiet.

Student Unrest At LHS Is Reported After Vote

Black student unrest at Lincolnton High School boiled over Monday afternoon after election of class officers for 1969-'70.

A crowd estimated at about 100 Negro students, mostly girls, gathered in the library of the school and loudly and profanely protested the results of the election which ended in white students being elected to office.

The Negroes charged the election had been rigged and made profane other remarks about it. They demanded a recount. Principal Jack Kiser was called and attempted to quiet the loudly shouting group. S. E. Biggers, president of the local NAACP organization, also was summoned and talked with the group urging them to quiet down. A Negro athlete picked out the more militant ones in the group and finally managed to quiet them down.

One girl, however, told Kiser that while they were leaving the matter wasn't going to be dropped. During conversation, she cussed.

Tuesday afternoon, more trouble started and acting on the demands of the black students there was a recount of the votes in the election. There was no change in the results. At this time the blacks had blocked doors leading into the auditorium. After some milling, shoving and loud talking the crowd broke up.

These are only two of several incidents that have occurred at the school during the current school year.

Kiser when questioned Wednesday morning about the incidents denied there had been any trouble. He said always after an election those who lose generally are dissatisfied and that goes for both white and black students. He said he had talked with "eight or 10" students. He said the only close election was for vice-president but that involved white students. He said no black student came close in the voting.

At no time this week were police called to try to quell the disturbance. However, they learned of trouble Monday and of the threat of further action and Tuesday were alerted to be ready if they should be called.

LINCOLN TIMES-NEWS

In what initially appeared to be the next crisis in the school, the elderly principal, Mr. Kiser, suffered chest pains and was rushed from school in an ambulance to the local hospital only to be diagnosed with . . . indigestion. His health problems were blamed by many of the white students and their parents on "all the pressure he's under because of the trouble the blacks are causing at Lincolnton High." To make matters even worse, the false rumor circulated that he had suffered a heart attack.

The flames were being fanned for a major confrontation when news unfolded that the KKK had decided to march in town to protest the "trouble that the blacks were causing" at the high school and to rally support for a countywide protest against the federally mandated integration of schools. The Klan had obtained a permit to march down Main Street and to hold a rally on the courthouse square on the day of the first football game of the season. Widely circulated among the whites was the additional rumor that, with the impending arrival of the Klan, the "blacks would start trouble."

A number of both black and white strangers from out-side the county began to appear in town. Black "agitators" were said to have been sent in by a northern civil rights group. It was generally agreed that the whites who were arriving from out of town were either Klan members them-selves or Klan supporters.

Boyce and I watched and listened and talked with each other about the situation melting down around us. Racial acrimony, especially with the potential for violence, was something strange and unfamiliar to us. I was sick that things had turned sour. I sensed a strained distance growing between me and many of my black friends, with the exception of Boyce. Our goodwill and friendship at school couldn't extend quite far enough to calm things down. Boyce and I talked about the problems that emerged, but at first, we had no conception of what might be done to help. We were afraid that conditions were apt to get worse, and we felt helpless.

I agreed with Boyce that the cheerleader selection had been unfair. In the matter of the school elections, a recount of the votes conducted with black students actually there to observe convinced them that they had been outnumbered legitimately, the vote drawn along racial lines.

One day after football practice, as Boyce and I were talking about the school crisis, the idea came to us that we both could go together to Mr. Kiser and ask that we be allowed to form a committee of both white and black students, male and female, so that we could try to "work things out on our own." With the white and black friends Boyce and I had, and with the goodwill formed among the players on the newly integrated football team, we figured we might have a chance to help if we could just get people talking to one another.

I contacted the principal, Mr. Kiser, whose indigestion was now under control, and presented the details of the plan that Boyce and I had worked out together. Mr. Kiser was skeptical, but he consented. "Well, I don't guess it'll hurt anything to give it a try. You two boys have to realize that we've got a bad situation here with the Klan coming. The mayor is even thinking about calling the governor to send the National Guard for the Klan march in case there's trouble. Frankly, I think that would just make things worse. That kind of attention is just what the Klan wants. We've already got enough police hanging around the school. With that paddy wagon in the parking lot, the police are just waiting for some sort of riot to break out. Having the police around here just seems to make everybody more nervous. Lord God, I don't know what's going to happen to this school. It seems they should have just left well enough alone. I think that's how most black and white folks feel."

With these words, Mr. Kiser acquitted me to work with Boyce to form the biracial committee. After football practice, Boyce and I drew up a list of black and white students who we thought would be the most respected and would have the most conciliatory influence on the others. With only three days before the football game and with the Klan reportedly intending to march the afternoon before the game, we needed to move quickly. We called around to enlist the committee members we had selected, and at school the next day, we held our first committee meeting during lunch period.

There were six black students on the committee, and I knew them all. The black girls were Shirley Bess and Chyral

Reinhardt. The black male students were Boyce, Ronnie Johnson, Nelson Wallace, and Sylvester Diamond, who seemed to be representing both himself and his sister Mary Jane.

The white male students were Scott Norwood, my fellow co-captain of the football team, Kim Rudisill, and Steve Suttle. True to the strong military tradition still respected in our town, Scott was bound for West Point, which the Confederate namesake of our high school had attended, and Steve was headed to the Coast Guard Academy. The two white girls on the committee were Kay Carpenter, a cheerleader, and Beverly Simmons, both of whom I had known since kindergarten in the Lutheran Church. Beverly, Kay, and I had been members of the same Lutheran confirmation class and had taken our first Communion together.

Chyral Reinhardt was the black girl whom I knew best on the committee, as she was good friends with a number of the Blake sisters. I now wonder if Chyral is distantly related to the Fesso, unknown hero of Ramsour's Mill. As was the custom, it is highly likely that Fesso and his children took the last name of his owner Christian Reinhardt. From reading the records of Victor Fair, Christian Reinhardt's great-great-grandson, I had gathered that in all likelihood, Fesso was granted his freedom following the Battle of Ramsour's Mill as reward for his faithful service to the Patriot cause. The possibility that Chyral was a distant descendent of Fesso is the type of irony that seems possible only in such a small place as Lincolnton.

Out of deference to the concerns of the black girls, who seemed most aggrieved, Boyce yielded co-chairmanship of the committee to Shirley Bess. The school's guidance counselor, Howard Parks, well-meaning and earnest, yet unbearably naive, had taken it upon himself to mediate the crisis and thus joined our first meeting. Parks never seemed to drop his air of peppy cheeriness, which had become particularly irritating to me under the present circumstances. I felt that he had no real grasp of how deep the resentments of the black students ran and no real conception of the legitimacy of their anger. I believe the word of choice today that would best describe him would be "clueless." I didn't trust him any more than the black students trusted him to handle this situation.

Parks attempted to start the meeting, which began in an atmosphere of uncertainty and uneasy silence while members of the committee wandered in with their lunches and found a place to sit around a large, square wooden table. Boyce and I sat beside each other, but the others divided themselves by color, blacks together, whites together. When Ronnie Johnson entered the room, he caught my eye and nodded his head in a silent token of recognition, the attitude of which I could not read. We had hardly spoken to each other since our fight in the pasture, which had occurred years ago. After that day, Ronnie had gradually drifted away from the various activities on Blake Hill.

Mr. Parks attempted to lighten the somber, uncomfortable feeling that dominated the room when he called the meeting to order, now that all committee members were gathered. "Well," he chirped, "it seems like we're all here. I would like to thank you all for coming to see what the problems are here at Lincolnton High and to try to figure out how we can work together to solve them. Now first, let me throw open the floor to discussion. Let's see what everyone's concerns are. Now, please feel free to just speak right up."

Parks did not know the black students, and vice versa. It was more than obvious that there was no black teacher included here. I assumed that the black guidance counselor at Newbold High either had lost his or her job or had been transferred elsewhere. No one really knew what had become of the former teachers of the black students. It was clear that all of the white teachers at LHS had stayed in place and that their jobs were secure.

What followed Parks's cheery opening remarks was sullen nonresponse. Boyce and I traded knowing glances as the excruciatingly long seconds passed. For one of us to break the ice would have been too easy in some way; we both wanted to see what the other black students had on their minds and to let them take the lead. The silence dragged on, and Parks apparently was not going break it, either. Committee members looked about the room, at the floor, at the ceiling, out the window, and at their shoes. Sylvester, who in many respects was quite shy, sat with his arms folded, staring at the floor. I tried to catch Ronnie Johnson's eye, and he seemed to sense my looking at him. He was the one who finally broke the silence, which, by now, had become pure torture.

Ronnie shifted about in his chair, then announced, "Yeah, I've got something to say, and I've got a problem." His voice was soft, yet serious. While the quiet had been ended at last, it was not relief that followed. Instead, the anxiety level increased in the room because all the black committee members present were familiar with the problems that Ronnie and I had had in the past. Only a few knew the details of our brief tussle in the pasture years ago, but those at the table were anxious about what he might say. When Ronnie began to speak, I saw Boyce shake his head and look at the floor. Neither of us could guess what might follow.

Parks, resuming his upbeat tone, encouraged him to continue: "Okay, now Ronnie, let's try to be as forthright and honest with each other as we can. We all want to hear what you have to say. Whatever the problem is, I'm just sure we can work it out if we work together."

"This is one problem I don't think anybody can fix," Ronnie resumed. His voice took on an overtly surly tone this time around. I saw Boyce's eyebrows furrow in puzzlement as he tried to read Ronnie's attitude. We thought we knew him pretty well, but he seemed for the moment to be inscrutable.

I was concerned that whatever he had to say could set the tone for the rest of the meeting and perhaps the outcome of our small committee's efforts at calming the seething anger that was pervading our school. I knew that Sylvester would be on my side, but he continued to sit with his arms folded and said nothing.

Parks chirped once again, "Now, Ronnie, I'm sure that whatever it is, we're going to do our best to fix it. Can you tell us about it?"

It seemed that Ronnie was deliberately allowing the tension and expectancy in the room to build. He was controlling the meeting and seemed to be enjoying it. I was becoming impatient. He glanced over at me, and I suddenly suspected that whatever he was about to say would be directed at me.

Briefly pointing in my direction with his thumb, he went on, "It's about Stoudemire over there." He paused, then added, "I've got a problem with Stoudemire." I saw a visible reaction of chagrin from Boyce as he looked up at the ceiling, then at me, and then stared at the floor. I sensed he was going to be careful and not choose sides. I glanced at Sylvester for help. He was frowning, and he directed the frown at Ronnie.

Parks, finally understanding he was not at a glee club organizational meeting, must have sensed that things could turn ugly here. He was nervous. The meeting was moving out of his control. Using his best reflective listening skill techniques, he embarrassingly parroted Ronnie's remark, "Now, Ronnie, it seems like you have a problem with Alan. Can you tell us more about it? I'm sure Alan would want to know."

Ronnie turned about and locked onto me with a glare. Several of the other students pulled back in their chairs into defensive positions as if readying themselves to clear the room for an impending fight between two rivals. Boyce remained silent. I think he knew, just as he did in the pasture that day, that I could hold my own. Still fixed squarely on me, Ronnie spoke again loud enough so that everyone would hear each word.

"I don't mind meeting with the other white kids here, but I can't sit here if I have to look at Stoudemire's ugly face." With that comment, I felt as if he had slapped a glove directly into my face. I had no idea how to respond. I sat without moving or speaking. Ronnie turned about to face Parks, now looking bewildered. Sylvester had unfolded his arms and placed his hands flat out on the table, as if he were about to jump out of his seat.

Following several additional excruciating seconds, Ronnie started up again, saying, "Well, I think I can explain something."

"Good!! Now, Ronnie, try to help us understand your feelings," opined Parks in a conspicuously shaky voice.

Ronnie took the cue. "Well, it's not exactly Zeke's fault." Then he paused, dragging out even longer the mystery he was creating.

"Now, Ronnie, who exactly is Zeke?" interjected Parks, who was thrown off base by the introduction of this new character.

Ronnie seemed surprised in having to explain the name "Zeke." Looking at the now even more confused Parks, he responded by saying simply, "Zeke is what all the black folk call Stoudemire over in Georgetown. It's a name Fox and his brothers gave him."

"And who is this Fox person, Ronnie? And where exactly is Georgetown?" Parks again inquired, aware he was moving rapidly out of his cultural territory.

Parks's interruption of Ronnie's performance with his never-ending questions due to his lack of knowledge about some basic facts here seemed to irritate Ronnie to the point that he lost all patience. "Never mind!" he insisted. "Just take it that Zeke is the same person you white folks call Alan Stoudemire. I'll tell you who Fox is some other time." Boyce smiled, and for the first time, I sensed that Ronnie was playing some sort of game with us, and I think Boyce sensed it, too.

Parks attempted to regain his balance, to keep the meeting going even if Ronnie was doing all the talking in his own taunting way. "Now, Ronnie," he begged again. If Parks said, "Now, Ronnie," one more time, I feared I would reach across the table and strangle him.

"Now, Ronnie, you said something about its not being Alan's, or, excuse me, Zeke's, fault. Can you explain what you mean?"

What Ronnie had been leading up to in his own calculated way was perfectly set up for him now. He was about to bring his contrived drama to a climax. Looking about the room, he started to speak. I detected what I interpreted as a bit of a smile, a slight upturn at the corners of his mouth, and an unmistakable twinkle in his eyes. Then he grinned.

"Well, it's like this. When Zeke's mama was praying for a baby, she asked the Lord to give her a snuggly little baby. Well, the Lord didn't hear her quite right and thought she'd asked for an ugly little baby. And that's what she got!!!"

With the punch line to the old joke finally delivered, Ronnie turned to me and broke out in a full, all-out smile. Then he began to laugh uncontrollably, slapping his hand down upon the table. Boyce had buried his head on the table and was convulsing with laughter as well. We'd been had. Ronnie had pulled off the perfect joke, and he was very much pleased with himself. Relieved as much as amused, the whole group, except for Parks, burst into giddy laughter, too, and it went on for several minutes. Parks managed a proper smile but appeared more confused than ever. Boyce raised his head and kept repeating amidst the laughter, "I should have seen it coming! I should have seen it coming! Lord have mercy!"

We calmed down, Ronnie stood up, reached across the table and extended his hand, which I readily grasped and shook. He then commented, "Now, Zeke, you know I didn't mean anything bad about your mama. You're the one with the ugly face!"

Smiling back at him, I retorted, "Yeah, and your mama's mama!" knowing that the phrase had no meaning, but served as a feeble, good-natured retaliation.

In Georgetown, to jokingly call someone "ugly" in the right circumstances signified teasing, adolescent affection. In one masterful stroke, Ronnie had buried an old hatchet between the two of us, broken the tension of the scene, and in his own clever way, brought our little group together that day. The event had additional significance because it immediately quelled the old gossip about the antipathy we had for each other. I still marvel at the heart and the subtle genius of his plan. From that point on, as one might imagine, the group became a cohesive one that worked quite well together, though, for Mr. Parks, I believe the reason for the transformation remained an enigma.

In fact, Mr. Parks, feigning composure, excused himself from the remainder of that first meeting, perhaps to reflect in solitude on the mystery of what had just occurred. Luckily for him, I did not have to hear, "Now, Ronnie . . ." again. Parks would have to wait to find out the true identity of the mysterious "Fox," as well as where to find Georgetown, which was not named on any official map.

With the ice thus broken, and by virtue of the fact that everyone on the committee grew almost immediately to like each other, we mutually decided to call the committee "Hand in Hand." No one recalls who first suggested that name for our group. It was mentioned early in the course of our discussions, and we settled on it as a name that seemed natural and friendly. We had a more official and bureaucratic name, as well. To the teachers and public, we were known as the "Student Relations Committee."

Our first order of business was to resolve the cheerleader problem. In what may have been the first affirmative action plan in America, initiated by a group of teenagers, planned and implemented on their own, our little committee arrived at the compromise proposal: From then on there should be selected for the squad of twelve a minimum number of black cheerleaders, which would match the percentage of black students attending the high school, with at least three black girls to be assured positions. In hopes of helping to calm down the disturbed and anxious town, we submitted a general announcement about the formation of the committee to the local *Lincoln Times,* which published it on the front page. Our report and the article read as follows:

The Student Relations Committee, Hand in Hand, has been formed with these purposes in mind:

I. To promote better understanding between students and teachers

2. To clear up any misunderstanding between the school and the general public

3. To serve as a grievance committee for all students of Lincolnton High School

4. To make recommendations to the faculty and administration on behalf of the students, which are subject to administration approval

Moreover, the Student Relations Committee has arrived at mutual agreements concerning our problems. The Committee recommends that:

1. There be no disciplinary action taken on incidents that took place before the Committee was founded.

2. We recommend to the student body that no further misconduct take place.

3. If any student has a grievance or problem, he or she should contact any member of the Committee and the problem will be brought before the Committee.

4. It is the desire of the Committee to solve any problems arising at Lincolnton High School before they become serious.

5. We, students of Lincolnton High School, and members of the Student Relations Committee feel it our duty to clear up the rumors the people of Lincolnton may have heard concerning the situation at our school. First, the majority of the

rumors being spread throughout the town are not true and have no factual basis. The several minor incidents that have occurred were mainly the result of personality differences and not the result of racial tensions. The black students presented their grievances peacefully and sensibly. Through class meetings and the organization of this committee, we hope to achieve unity among all students of Lincolnton High School.

HAND in HAND

A progress report from the Student Relations Committee, Second Session.

The Student Relations Committee met to discuss problems concerning students of Lincolnton High.

The first problem brought before the committee was that of bus transportation. A sub-committee was formed to gather information concerning school bus integration, bus routes, and walking distances to the bus stops. The sub-committee will report to the SRC at the next meeting.

The second topic of discussion was the selection of cheerleaders. More information was needed, and the problem will be discussed at a future date.

The Student Relations Committee again invites any student who has a complaint or problem to bring it to the attention of the committee. Any problem brought before the committee in this manner will be fully discussed and a course of action will be recommended.

Co-Chairmen: Shirley Bess and Alan Stoudemire

Please post and read to homeroom class.

HAND in HAND

A progress report from the Student Relations Committee.

Fourth Report

The Student Relations Committee met at 9:30 a.m.

The cheerleader constitution was drawn up by the cheerleaders and was read and distributed by the committee. This was the main order of business.

The constitution was drawn up by the cheerleaders themselves and the faculty. The new advisor is Mrs. Gilleland.

The SRC made the following recommendations for the New Cheerleader Constitution:

(1) That the academic grade average be lowered to 75.

(2) That supplies for posters (etc.) be supplied by the school for the cheerleaders.

(3) That transportation to and from away games be supplied by the school.

It must be stated that these are only recommendations, and must be either accepted or rejected by the administration and faculty.

An open invitation remains for the students to air their problems and gripes through the SRC.

Please post and read to homeroom class.

HAND in HAND

Fifth progress report from the Student Relations Committee.

The SRC gave its approval to the New Cheerleader Constitution.
It should be noted that the constitution provides for the selection of
cheerleaders from a bi-racial group of cheerleaders from outside
our conference. The minimum academic grade average for
participation remains at 80.

Through recommendations by the SRC, 4 additional Negro sopho-
mores were added to the waiter-waitress group for the Jr.-Sr.

Two letters were written to the Administration suggesting formally
that the following matters be considered: (1) The possibility of
hiring more Negro teachers in the future and (2) The possibility
of offering an elective course in Negro history for all students
and (3) The possibility of adding more books to the library
pertaining to Negro history and interests.

The SRC also takes this opportunity to recommend to the faculty
that Seniors who average 90 or above on a subject be exempt from
the Final Examination on that subject.

On the subject of Student dress code, it was felt that if the
existing rules are enforced, that no additional rules or guidelines
are necessary.

We would like to clear up any rumors concerning whether or not the
SRC had anything to do with the color of this year's annuals. We
did not. Honest.

All recommendations of the SRC are only suggestions, which are
subject to either approval or rejection by the party to whom they are
addressed to.

HAND in HAND

A progress report from the Student Relations Committee.
Sixth report.

The SRC met with Mr. Propst to discuss the recent recommendations made to the administration concerning the following topics:

(1) Negro history course. Mr. Propst informed the committee that a letter had been written to the State Department of Public Instruction concerning information on Negro history courses. Mr. Propst said that any course would have to be approved by the State before the local administration could give approval to such a course. This is all that can be done at the present time.

Mr. Propst did inform the SRC that a supplement entitled "The Negro in American History" will be added to the 11th grade history course next year. This supplement brings out and emphasizes the Negro role in American history.

(2) The hiring of Negro teachers. Mr. Propst said that teachers were hired on the basis of their ability only. He also said that of 25 applications for teaching positions received for next year only 2 were from Negro teachers. Selection of teachers is also based on their ability to teach a subject for which a vacancy occurs. Any teacher that is hired is selected on a purely fair basis.

(3) Negro literature in the library. Mr. Propst said that a bibliography would be prepared listing all such books available in the library. Miss Stroupe informed him that certain Negro magazines available at Newbold last year have been subscribed to for next year.

The Student Relations Committee would like to thank Mr. Propst and the rest of the administration for their interest and concern.

The SRC discussed how the Committee would be selected next year. Further discussion is necessary and the Student Body will be informed of the final outcome and plan. It can be assumed that the Committee will be a sub-committee of the Student Council and consist of both elected and appointed members.

While it was several days before the first of these simple documents was published and circulated among the student body, we presented it and the cheerleader selection plan to the principal the next day. Mr. Kiser thanked us for what we had tried to do to calm things down and said he thought our plan "sounds reasonable," but he added, "I'll have to run this by the teachers and coaches first."

When approval of the plan was announced, a collective sigh of relief seemed to pass through the school. While tensions at the school dissipated slowly, another crisis in the community loomed ahead. The Klan was still planning to march in a few days to protest school integration.

When we hung up our practice uniforms the day before the big football game with Rutherfordton High School, Boyce remarked to me, "What about the Klan, Zeke? I've heard pretty much for sure there's going to be trouble when they march, and it won't take much to start it. I've heard some talk, and it isn't good, I can tell you that."

I had already given the problem some thought as the week leading up to the football game and Klan march approached. Concern had grown among the whites about the impending appearance of the KKK, and the black community was angry and understandably threatened by them, too. In the midst of the brewing trouble, Boyce and I continued to talk. We developed a plan.

The fateful Friday arrived when the Klan was to march around four in the afternoon. I had heard that the Klansmen were to don their uniforms in a secretive place just outside of town behind an old, closed-down mill. As their ominous, slow march down Main Street got underway, they must have expected the usual police lines, jeering from blacks who had the nerve to watch, and cheers from white redneck supporters waving Confederate flags. Typically, I have heard, there would be in the crowd others who came just to "see if the Klan still really existed."

Unlike the usual scene awaiting the Klan, however, Main Street was surprisingly empty. The one hundred or so Klansmen were met by only a few citizens, black and white, standing about, gawking in silence at their parade. A few city policemen were standing about, too; the mayor had not bothered calling in the local National Guard, which the KKK surely took as a disappointment. The mayor, like Principal Kiser, must have appreciated that to have the KKK conclude that their presence warranted military intervention would only make them feel more powerful. The sparse crowd who showed up that day seemed to be there more out of curiosity than for any other reason.

The Klan continued to march down East Main Street toward the courthouse in their silver robes and white hoods. Before long, they must have begun hearing from a distance the sound of music coming from a crowd of young people gathered about the court square lawn at the end of Main

Street, which was the terminus of their march. When the Klansmen marched closer, they couldn't help but see that the crowd was a mixed group of black and white teenagers.

Soon they were close enough to recognize the lively sounds as "beach music," the same music played by groups like the Tams and the Four Tops at large dance pavilions like the ones at Myrtle Beach, South Carolina. The music boomed from a large radio positioned on the top step leading up to the courthouse and was tuned to a popular station. The Klan beheld our festive, spirited group talking, mingling about, and clearly enjoying one another. Rather than intimidating anyone according to the Klan's intention, their parade assumed a circuslike atmosphere. There were no bitter or angry calls to them from the black students. They, along with the white students, found the disguised, oaflike figures buffoonish curiosities in their ghostly garb. We looked to see whether we could recognize any locals under the hoods.

Boyce and I had rounded up most of the members of the football team, both black and white. The male members of our "Hand in Hand" school committee were there, not exactly "hand in hand," but standing there, nonetheless, side by side, shoulder to shoulder, black and white. Sylvester Diamond had convinced his sister Mary Jane to join us. The crowd was about equally mixed, black and white, but in spite of my best efforts, no white girls had agreed to join the group. Most of those I had urged to come explained that the situation was "too dangerous" or that their parents wouldn't allow them to come.

As the Klan neared us, it slowed its pace, doubtless trying to figure out why this group of black and white teenagers was assembled. We could see them better now. Then something happened that threatened to cause the day to explode.

From behind our crowd, I noticed that none other than Tanker Sherrill had shown up. We had suspected him to be among the hooded White Knights. He shuffled slowly through our group to the front, still a significant distance from Boyce and me. We craned our necks to watch his next step. We were very curious to see what he was doing here. Those who spotted his presence, both black and white students, stood aside to let him pass. With him were several of his friends, who were hanging behind him at some distance. It did not appear his buddies wanted to be a part of whatever Tanker had planned.

As Tanker negotiated his way slowly toward the front of the crowd, I could see that he was heading directly for Mary Jane Diamond. Boyce grabbed my arm and pulled me over closer to Mary Jane, who was standing several feet away. Sylvester had noticed Tanker, too, and, preparing for any harassment of his sister that Tanker might have in mind, he, too, had moved closer. The circle widened around Tanker, and conversations stopped. It looked like trouble was about to erupt again between Tanker and Mary Jane. Meanwhile, the

Klan members were taking note of what looked like an emerging black-white confrontation. They had stopped their march to watch and waited like vultures from the sidelines.

About ten feet behind Mary Jane, Tanker, his hands in his pockets, called out above the music, "Mary Jane! Mary Jane!" Mary Jane had become aware of his presence, but, until now, she had chosen to ignore him.

Mary Jane turned around. Evidently expecting the worst from him, she instinctively thrust her hand in the purse slung about her shoulder, where we all knew she would find her infamous straight razor. I looked about to see if there were any policemen nearby. There were none in sight.

Without hesitation, Mary Jane marched fearlessly up to Tanker, who stood his ground. He only glanced at her, then stared at his feet and shuffled them about. He looked nervous.

Mary Jane took the initiative. Moving within inches of Tanker's face, she needled him, "Tanker Sherrill, haven't you had enough, white boy? You got a lot of nerve showing up here like this. We were all looking for you out there with your buddies in the Klan."

Mary Jane was visibly angry. It would take only a slight false move or wrong word from Tanker, and her razor would be slashing across his face. We watched intensely to see what Sylvester would do, but he was standing back, keeping his distance, apparently having decided to let the drama play out on its own.

Tanker, still looking at his feet, finally responded in a quavering, barely audible voice, "I came here to tell you something, Mary Jane."

"Like what? To tell me they're having a sale on bananas and watermelons at the grocery store? I've had enough of what you've got to say, Tanker, and you know damn well I'm not taking any more lip from your smart mouth!"

Tanker, now avoiding altogether any eye contact with her, mumbled something that the rest of us could not hear. Mary Jane looked puzzled, too, and asked, "What did you say, Tanker? Did I hear you right, boy?"

Tanker spoke up a little; someone had turned off the radio, so we could hear better what they were saying to each other. It was very quiet.

"I said I came here to tell you I was sorry about what I said the other day at school. I was just runnin' my mouth, like usual. You can cut me if you want to, Mary Jane. I probably deserve it, but I don't want any more trouble, and I just came to say I'm sorry."

With his head cast down, he still wasn't looking at anyone. Mary Jane appeared dumbfounded, but it was unlikely that anything could catch her off guard for long. Even Mary Jane must have seen that Tanker, in spite of himself and for whatever reason, was trying to do something right for a change.

The puzzled expression faded from her face. She pulled her hand out of her purse, and it was empty. She moved closer to Tanker, and, whereas Tanker was slightly taller than she, they stood now almost nose to nose.

With squinted eyes and a tightly drawn face, Mary Jane would surely unload on Tanker now that he was in such a vulnerable and humiliating position. Even though Mary Jane was staring straight at him, Tanker would not look up at her. Then Mary Jane spoke in a voice loud enough for all around them, including several of the Klan members who had slipped in closer amidst our gathering, to hear. "You know what you are, Tanker Sherrill? Do you really want to know what you are?" she demanded of him.

Mary Jane waited for a response. Tanker looked defeated and only answered, "Whatever you say, Mary Jane. Whatever you say."

Her face then broke into a broad and bright smile. She put her hand on Tanker's right shoulder in an openly affectionate manner. She repeated loud enough for everyone to hear once again, "You know what you are, Tanker? . . . You're a mess! You're just one big ol' mess!"

In those days, calling someone "a mess," like the careful use of "ugly," was all but a sign of affection. Tanker smiled and glanced up to see Mary Jane grinning at him. Somewhat disbelieving the drama we had just witnessed, we all began to relax and shake our heads in amazement.

For Tanker Sherrill to apologize, and for Mary Jane to forgive him, in her own way, seemed nothing short of a miracle.

Tanker slowly backed away while Mary Jane still grinned at him. Then he turned and began to walk in the direction of his car. He glanced briefly over his shoulder and said, "All right, Mary Jane, I'll see you around." He turned again and walked away, avoiding everyone.

Having been completely absorbed by the encounter between Mary Jane and Tanker, we noticed that the Klan was nowhere in sight. Disappointed, no doubt, in the puzzling reconciliation they had just witnessed, defeated in their mission to stir up anger and protest, they had limped on around the courthouse. Most of us were close to speechlessness and could only share words like "amazing" and "unbelievable." The music was cranked up again, and, pondering the small wonder that had just occurred, we drifted apart.

Those of us on the football team headed to the other side of the courthouse toward the old North State Hotel. It was nearly time for the pregame meeting, and our team dinner was to be held at the old hotel, which stood just across from the courthouse square. The Klan members had vanished.

The day of the parade now seems like a strange dream. I remember little about the game that night other than the fact that we won it by a score of 7–0. A new halfback by the name of Boyce Blake scored the only touchdown of the game.

The rest of our senior year passed quickly. We did not win the state championship because we lost the big game of the year to our archrival Shelby High. After we lost that game, I felt high school was essentially over for me. When spring came that year, Boyce and I ran on the track team together. After graduation, we both took full-time jobs in textile mills for the summer and saw little of each other. I was still dating Mary, who would be attending the local community college, the same one that Boyce was planning to attend in the fall. Sam had been drafted, and Tom had volunteered for the air force. It was 1969, and the worst of Vietnam was still to come.

One day later that summer, I would finally leave the farm and Lincolnton. I can still remember the directive my father gave me as we drove away from the farm that day: "You might be from the country, but you don't have to act like it."

I recall looking back over my shoulder through the dust created by the wheels of our car as we drove the half mile of dirt road from our house. I watched the surrounding woods and Blake Hill slowly recede. I wanted one last glimpse of the south range of the Blue Ridge Mountains, whose gentle and comforting outline were clearly visible from the high pasture that overlooked our farm. When I looked back, my dog Whitey was chasing after the car as if he knew he was being left behind for good.

Sunrise over Carolina

> Sorrow tarrieth for the night,
> But joy cometh in the morning.
>
> —Psalm 30:5

During the intervening years, my irregular visits home caused me to all but lose track of Boyce and his brothers. I had finished college, medical school, and in spite of a serious bout with cancer during my internship after medical school, I had completed my residency training program in psychiatry. I entered academia at Duke and then became well ensconced as a professor of psychiatry at Emory University School of Medicine in Atlanta. I was on the fast track and rarely traveled home to Lincolnton. All the Blake brothers had scattered from Blake Hill, and I did not have the time on my brief holiday visits home to track them all down. I heard that Boyce had a daughter, Vonetta, by his first wife and had remarried and fathered by his second wife Rita, a son called B.J., which I assumed stood for "Boyce Junior." Otherwise, I knew little of the details of his adult life.

None of the black students from our senior year attended our high school reunions that were held every five years—not surprising, since at least several of these reunions had been held at the VFW building. In spite of all of the years that had gone by, it still remained a symbol of segregation, and as far as I knew, it remained all-white as did the infamous pool, which had finally been shut down. The concrete of the pool was cracked and deteriorated, and the basin of the pool itself was full of dirt and sand and overgrown with weeds. A new city pool had been built in town and was completely integrated. It was the first time that the blacks of the county had anywhere to swim other than the creeks and the river.

Then several things happened that jolted me from my plans to continue to climb the professional ladder of medicine, a career path that seemed well laid out for me, given my steady record of success as a teaching and practicing psychiatrist. My mother called me one night to tell me that she had heard from Boyce, who was trying to find me. He had told her that he had been diagnosed with Lou Gehrig's disease. The painful memory of my mother's telephone call is still vivid for me. Lou Gehrig's disease is one of the most dreaded conditions in all of medicine. With this disease, the nervous system, for unknown reasons, begins to degenerate, beginning with the peripheral muscles of the legs and hands, then progressing towards the central part of the body. Eventually, every muscle is completely paralyzed, including the breathing muscles, at which point patients, who are usually unable even to swallow, are put on a ventilator. They are then completely helpless. There is no known cause or cure. From start to finish, the disease progresses to death in three or four years, at best.

I hung up the telephone with my mother, stunned, and finding the news difficult to comprehend, I immediately called Boyce. In almost every way, in spite of the circumstances, it was the same old Fox. He sounded calm and steady, which was remarkable, yet so typical of him. I found him to be almost optimistic, if not unrealistic. There was not a trace of self-pity in his voice.

It did not take us long to catch up on news of our families. I insisted that he let me arrange to have him see a neurologist at Emory, where I practiced and taught. I had not accepted the diagnosis and felt he should have, in any case, a second opinion. Besides, there were experts in the area of Lou Gehrig's disease on the faculty at Emory. The unfairness of his situation made me both sad and sick. I took it upon myself to try to undo somehow what I knew was to be not just a fatal diagnosis, if it were true, but a long and miserable process of dying.

Boyce came to Emory for his appointment, as I had arranged, but I was out of town at a professional meeting and missed him the day he was there. Upon my return, I called the neurologist who had evaluated him, and he confirmed the diagnosis. Again, I experienced that same sinking feeling that was mixed with anger and helplessness. When I talked to Boyce about the confirming bad news, he did not sound surprised or even sad. He had already accepted what I could not. He knew he was going to die.

I had cared for patients with Lou Gehrig's disease in my own practice, but I had never cared for anyone close to me with the disease. I knew what lay in store for Boyce, and I dreaded it for him. I reassured him that I would help him make whatever medical decisions were necessary. He insisted that he never be put on a respirator, and I promised him I would make sure his wishes were followed. I found a childhood acquaintance, Rob Reid, practicing as a family doctor in Lincolnton, to take over his day-to-day care. I referred him to Johnathan Rhyne, a lawyer in Lincolnton, a classmate from our senior year at Lincolnton High, who helped him draw up a will and get his affairs in order. I also set up an educational trust fund for B.J., made my own contribution to it, and solicited contributions from some of our old friends. Scott Norwood, my fellow co-captain on the football team, who had become a trauma surgeon in Texas after serving with distinction as a surgeon in the military, made one of the most generous donations. My mother-in-law donated another generous gift of stock, and before long, the trust was completely endowed. Knowing that B.J. was assured a college education seemed to give Fox great peace of mind. I could tell the most painful part of his illness was knowing that he was going to have to leave B.J. behind. I told Fox that whatever happened, I would take care of B.J., who was seven years old, if, for any reason, his wife, Rita, was unable to do so.

I didn't know B.J. very well, but I do remember the first time we saw each other, just a few years before. I had pulled into the driveway at Blake Hill, and Miss Ruth and a number of the other Blakes who were about the place walked out to greet me. Boyce introduced me to B.J. and suggested he shake my hand. B.J. hesitated. He must have been about five years old then. Fox looked down at B.J. and said, "B.J., this is Zeke. You remember me telling you about how Zeke and me grew up together, don't you?"

A puzzled look came over B.J.'s face as he warily shook my hand. Then he looked at his father and said, "Daddy, that can't be Zeke!"

Equally puzzled, his father asked him while glancing at me, "B.J., what's wrong with you, boy? Why can't that be Zeke?"

B.J. looked at me again and then turned back to his father. "I thought Zeke was a black boy. You never said nothin' about him being a white boy!" Our puzzlement was transformed into laughter, which did not help to clear up B.J.'s confusion.

Then Miss Ruth, who had been standing to the side listening, turned to me and said, "Well, Lord have mercy! All these years, B.J. thought you was black! Well, you might as well have been one of my own. You spent so much time over here, I always set an extra plate at the table 'cause I never knew when you'd show up for supper. You boys were some kind of mess, I tell you that!!" In his own small way, B.J. had captured the very essence of our friendship.

All of our good memories could not cover up the present situation. Boyce and I talked on the telephone at least twice a week after that, sometimes about straightening out his financial and legal matters and about B.J.'s trust fund. At other times, we just talked about old times and relived the days on the creek, in the pasture playing softball, and our glory days of high school football at Battleground Stadium. We kept planning to get our old Georgetown friends together for another game of bid whiz the next time I was home. The game was to be postponed indefinitely.

In November 1996, only a year after learning of Boyce's diagnosis of Lou Gehrig's disease, I was again struck by cancer. In some ways, it was not a surprise, but I had mistakenly thought that one case of cancer was enough for a lifetime.

With the second cancer diagnosis, I was given a 10 percent chance of being alive in two years. I looked back at my childhood, my family, my marriage, and my career, which, according to statistics, was to be suddenly cut short.

I thought back over everything that had happened to us since that day on the courthouse lawn when the Klan had marched. I remembered Boyce's spectacular game-winning touchdown that same night against Rutherfordton. I thought of the victory celebration we enjoyed in fits of laughter along with Mary Jane's brother Sylvester in the locker room after the game. Sylvester, muddy and bloodied by the brutal battle, had embraced me with a crushing hug, and, in jubilation, he had shouted, "I love you, Zeke! I love you, man!" I knew he meant it.

We went on to have a winning season that year, with a record of 9–1, even though, for that football season, the cheerleading squad remained all-white. New cheerleaders were selected for the next year according to our grievance committee's plan. This change would occur only after Fox, Sylvester, and the rest of the seniors, including myself, had graduated, said our farewells on graduation night, and gone our separate ways.

Following graduation, Boyce stayed in Lincolnton and intermittently attended a few years of community college. In his early twenties, he married his first wife with whom he had his daughter. He went to work in a factory that made cardboard boxes, and over the years, he had become a well-respected supervisor, Sunday school teacher and star player on his company's softball team. One of our football teammates that year, Maurice Moore, "De Maurice," as we called him, had joined the Army and had won the Army championship in karate. Maurice was the middle-weight Inter-service boxing champion, European kick-boxing champion, and the European semi-contact karate champion. He has also acted in a number of Hollywood martial arts films. When Maurice came home, he opened up a karate studio, where Boyce was spending more and more time. Maurice now had two children in college and another in law school. One of his daughters became an attorney, another an F.B.I. agent, and both sons played college basketball on scholarships.

Since leaving for college, I had lived in Chapel Hill, North Carolina, where I studied medicine; Denver, Colorado, where I completed my medicine internship and residency in psychiatry; Durham, North Carolina, where I served as a faculty member at Duke Medical School; and finally Atlanta, Georgia, where I taught and directed a combined medical/psychiatry unit at Emory University Medical School. Boyce remained in Lincolnton. He had earned a third-degree black belt at Maurice's gym and had become a part-time instructor there himself. He had followed the religious inclinations so evident in his youth and become an active and respected member of the Second Baptist Church of Lincolnton, where he taught Sunday school. The First Baptist Church was, of course, all-white, as it had always been.

While Boyce was getting on with his life in Lincolnton, I had married at age twenty-five during medical school, won over by my college sweetheart, Sue Sprunt, who was to see me through my first bout of cancer and would stand by me through the terrors that awaited in the years to come. I remember being smitten immediately by her demure and charming kindness and innocence the very first time I saw her when we were twenty-one. Her red hair, fair skin, blue-green eyes, and slightly freckled face came from her direct Scottish ancestry. When I brought her home to meet my parents, I also took her to meet Boyce. He called me later and gave me his unequivocal stamp of approval. "That's a fine girl, Zeke, but you better marry her quick before she finds out what you're really like!" With Boyce's approval, I followed his advice, and we were married soon thereafter two hundred miles away in Sue's mother's hometown of Raleigh.

When my cancer first struck me at age twenty-seven, it manifested itself as a pain in my right knee. I was less than two years into my marriage, and less than a year out of medical school, a young, insecure intern at the University of Colorado Medical School, preparing for my psychiatric residency. When I finally had the painful leg formally evaluated in the middle of my internship year, the diagnosis was made swiftly and decisively. It was a rare form of bone cancer.

My doctors made it clear that the only way to stop the cancer was to amputate above the knee. Before I really knew what was happening, I was wheeled into a surgery that would change my life forever. I was two thousand miles away from home and feeling very alone.

My amputation had been not only painful, but humiliating. The amputation was a castration of my sense of myself as a person and as a man. I also felt humiliated and ashamed by the loss of all my hair during the ten months of chemotherapy that followed.

In spite of the amputation and threat of death that hung over me like the sword of Damocles, I did what my father would have done: I returned to work. Four weeks after the amputation and just a few days after my first round of chemotherapy, I was working in the emergency room of Denver University Hospital on crutches. I had not been fitted for a prosthesis. The ability to work was in many ways my salvation. The harder and longer I worked, the less time I had to think about what I had lost or about my chances of survival, which was uncertain at the time. I worked, and my life and my training proceeded.

The chemotherapy required hospitalization for a week out of each month and consisted of four highly toxic drugs, which I received intravenously. I would work at the hospital for three weeks, then take a week off for the treatments. I remembered chemotherapy as an excruciatingly miserable and frightening experience. It was not just the trauma of the surgery and the debilitating effects of the chemotherapy;

cancer robbed me of any sense of security about life. I was always terrified that the cancer could return at any time without warning. This fear would never leave me.

The chemotherapy, designed to prevent any spread of the bone tumor, worked, but the cure had been bought at the price of hours and hours of intractable nausea and violent retching that would leave me exhausted, dehydrated, debilitated, and depressed. In the midst of the chemotherapy, I struggled to adapt to the artificial leg, a miserable contraption that I viewed as a pathetic substitute for my real leg. I was ashamed of the wooden leg, just as I was ashamed of my mutilated body and barely disguised, ill-fitting wig.

Sue not only stood by me in the midst of the most frightening news of my cancer diagnosis, but during endless hours of emptying basins of vomit and the vile and stinking contents of bedside commodes for the duration of the ten months of chemotherapy. I knew that she would be there for me for any reason, at any time, until the bitter end, regardless of how bitter and lonely that end might be. I had found what all men seek, the complete love and devotion of one true heart. I knew I was extraordinarily lucky to have her.

In spite of Sue's faithful support, the sense of being sick, frightened, all but alone, and so far away from all that was familiar to me made the pain and loneliness of that cancer battle even worse. I was, however, determined to stick it out, to complete the chemotherapy, and to finish my four-year residency in psychiatry. I wanted to go home, but felt that if I did, it would be a sign of weakness. I had made it to the big city, to a prestigious residency program, and I would be damned if I would let the cancer take that away from me. I nevertheless longed to see my friends, my family, and to once again enjoy the friendliness and familiarity of the small town. My feelings about home were fraught with ambivalence. It was not that I could not go home again. I would not let myself go home.

Fox was one of the first of the few people to call me after my leg was amputated. He said to me, "Zeke, hold your head up, man! When you come home, we'll play some bid whiz. You don't need but one leg for that anyway, and maybe you can hide some aces for us in that wooden one they gonna give you!"

I did visit home after the surgery and in the midst of chemotherapy. I asked Sue to drive me over to Blake Hill to see if I could find Boyce, Tom, or Johnny. As we drove up the hill, I remember the first thing I saw as we rounded the top of the hill and pulled into their yard. Under the same apple tree where we had played so many card games and where I had made my moonshine debut, sat Johnny, Sam, and Boyce playing cards. Without much ado, they looked up, flashed their ever-ready friendly smiles, and Boyce called out, "Zeke! Where you been, man? We've been saving a place for you!" With a minimum of surprise or sentiment, they moved aside and made a place for me at the table. They now had a fourth hand for a game of bid whiz.

Miss Ruth appeared, came over and gave me a hug. "Zeke! Lord have mercy! Where have you been, child?" Without waiting for a response, she set down on the table a glass of lemonade. The fact that she was permitting us to play cards in public was a major concession on her part, thus making me feel the welcome home was even more special.

Before she left, she said to my wife, "Now, I guess I can leave these boys alone for a while. . . ." She paused for dramatic effect, then added, "if you'll watch them." All of us laughed. "The last time I left them home, Zeke here managed to get himself into a mess of trouble!" she cackled. With that comment, I knew that Punkin had betrayed me. While the other Blake brothers were howling in laughter remembering that day under the apple tree, Miss Ruth turned and pointed an arthritic finger straight at Johnny, who instantly became quiet. "And you, Mr. Johnny Blake, I'll personally keep an eye on you! Don't you think you're too big for me to take a switch to you!" Johnny remained respectfully quiet knowing, while Miss Ruth was teasing him, he better not take any chances with her.

She then turned to me and asked, "Did you know, Zeke, I found out about that race he had with that white boy from Victory Grove?" Without waiting for an answer from me, she went right on. "Yes, indeed, I did. . . ."

It didn't matter that the race had been more than ten years ago. Johnny was still in for one more lecture. She headed toward the house, then backed up a bit to address me again. "Now, Zeke, don't you be a stranger 'round here. You been gone too long as it is." With that, she left, and we began the bidding. I was home, and it felt good. If I saw Punkin, I would demand that she reimburse me for the ten or so Moon Pies that I thought had bought her silence. She had some reckoning to do. Punkin was married and had moved off Blake Hill with her husband, but not so far away that I could not look her up.

I returned to Colorado after this short stay at home and, with great relief, finally finished the chemotherapy. Then I waited in further agony from month to month to see if the chest X-rays and bone scans revealed any return of the cancer. In spite of my worst fears, I remained cancer-free and struggled to complete my residency amidst obsessive fear and dread of a relapse. My hope gradually grew back with my hair and my growing confidence in the stability and fit of my artificial leg.

I finished my training, and, regardless of the frightening cancer experience, life and my marriage went on. Sue and I had two children, a girl and a boy. Anna, born in 1981, inherited much of my own personality. She is prone to worry and take life too seriously. She holds a faint hint of melancholy under the surface. Sometimes I blame myself for these traits, as I feel she may have absorbed some of my own pain and depression in the early years of our marriage. She was born only three years after my initial cancer surgery.

She is a beautiful young girl, however, who carries herself with the same demure manner as her mother. She has smooth and flawless skin even as a teenager, large, chocolate-brown eyes, and a faint olive tinge to her dark skin, a hallmark of many of the women on my father's side of the family. She is fiercely independent and has a will of iron that as a small child was often mistaken for simple stubbornness, a characteristic likely due to her Scottish genes. Committed to values and causes, she possesses a maturity rare for her age, rare for any age, for that matter.

Like Anna, our son Will possesses a wonderful mix of personality characteristics. Born in 1984, Will has a sunny, easy-going disposition. Full of humor and goodwill, he manages to have a good time in almost any circumstance. I think he picked up some of these characteristics from me, which, in turn, I believe I learned from the Blakes. With a gift for friendship, Will is gentle, openhearted, and kind. He is also bright and possesses a great deal of intellectual curiosity. This curiosity, along with his adventuresome spirit, has led him to pursue rock climbing as a hobby, ecological study in the most primitive of settings in Costa Rica, and marine biology study on North Carolina's Outer Banks. Physically agile and strong, and loving athletics like I did at his age, he runs cross-country and pole-vaults and is an award-winning wrestler for his school.

Largely because of the medical trauma I experienced, I specialized in medical psychiatry, a small subspecialty that focuses on the psychological and emotional care of patients with physical disease, such as cancer, heart disease, and neurological disorders. This treatment was generally missing for these patients, whose psychiatric condition was marked by overwhelming fear, anxiety, and depression. I set up a model hospital program to care for such patients and published a number of textbooks on their diagnosis and treatment." I managed to garner a modest national reputation for myself in this area and helped establish similar programs at other hospitals across the country.

Everything seemed to be on track. I was confident that after eighteen years, I was completely safe from any return of the bone cancer. I had a good marriage, a more than successful career, two good-hearted, beautiful, and talented children, and no financial problems. Too, I had decided to get myself in good physical shape by using a rowing machine and lifting weights. Except for my high school years when I was playing football and running track, I was in the best shape of my life, or so I thought.

About a year after Boyce was diagnosed with Lou Gehrig's disease, I passed out while exercising in my basement on November 2, 1996. Following an ambulance trip to the local hospital and scans, the devastating news was delivered: I had a brain tumor. It turned out to be melanoma, malignant skin cancer that had spread to my brain, lungs, and other parts of my body.

After the initial shock of the diagnosis had worn off, I became severely depressed. My worst nightmare had been fulfilled. It was not so much death that I feared, but more chemotherapy and the process of dying from cancer, and most of all, leaving my family.

Neurosurgery was successful in removing the cancerous nodule in the brain, and I again embarked on the rigors of chemotherapy combined with several immunotherapy drugs, designed to stimulate my own immune system to fight against the cancer.

The chemotherapy was less toxic this time, primarily due to new medications that worked remarkably well in controlling the nausea and vomiting. Six months of chemotherapy seemed to control the spread of the cancer, but it had not reduced the size of the tumor nodules in the lungs. I entered an experimental therapy program, also designed to activate my own immune system against the cancer, and initially, it seemed to go beyond containing the cancer to reducing it somewhat. My neurosurgery and the frequency of my treatments prevented me from returning to work. Ironically, for the first time in my life, when I was not in the hospital or otherwise ill from treatment, I had my first opportunity to write in an unfettered way. I would call this time my "melanoma sabbatical."

Fox and I continued to talk regularly now that we both were ill. As Boyce had put it in one of many conversations, "Well, Zeke, we've done come full circle. We started out together, and now we've come back together again. We might as well go out together if we have to. But let's hang in there together while we can, partner."

Although we never directly expressed it to each other, as it was not our way, we shared a deep bond of affection and respect for each other. We were drawn even closer by our illnesses. It helped to be facing sickness with a close friend. The sharing decreased the sense of isolation that accompanies almost all serious illnesses.

It was odd how Boyce found out I was ill again. Just two days after I fell unconscious, due to the tumor, Boyce by chance came to Emory for a follow-up visit in the neurology clinic, after which we had planned to go out to eat. He called my office looking for me, and my secretary had given him the news. I was in another hospital at the time, and under the circumstances, I had forgotten our planned rendezvous. Boyce had to return home that day with whoever had provided him with transportation from Lincolnton, which was a four-hour drive from Atlanta. It was several weeks before I felt strong enough to call him and catch him up on my bad news.

Boyce's remarkable acceptance and continuing ability to find quiet contentment in life confounded me. In sharp

contrast to Boyce's calm acceptance of his fate, I was infuri-
ated. I had already had cancer once, and once was enough.
What had I done to deserve this? I was bitter and anxious.
To make matters more frustrating, my doctors could find no
primary source of the tumor. There were no malignant moles
to be found on my skin. Having developed into a cancer pho-
bic, I had seen a dermatologist regularly and had insisted
compulsively over the years that even the smallest mole that
looked too dark or irregular be removed. In spite of my dili-
gence, I had developed melanoma anyway from an unknown
site. There seemed to be nothing I could do to escape my
genetic destiny. I had escaped once, but not this time. I felt
fated to make my rendezvous with this deadly disease.

I set about putting my own affairs in order, expecting
the worst. I changed my own will to add to B.J.'s trust fund
to make sure there would be enough for him to go to any college he wanted to attend. I made sure that Boyce had a living
will that clearly stated his wishes for his terminal care in case
I wasn't around when it came to that.

The last few times I visited him at home in Lincolnton,
he knew he would die soon, and he would tell me, "Zeke, you
know I'm just tired, man. I'm ready to go." He spent much of
his time listening to gospel music. He had become almost
completely paralyzed, unable to feed or to bathe himself.
Whenever I called him, his wife, Rita, or B.J. held the telephone up to his ear so that he could talk. His hands, the same

ones that had once earned him the third-degree black belt in karate, were now too weak to accomplish even this simple task. Lou Gehrig's was a miserable disease, and I despised it.

I mourned for Boyce, and I mourned for our child-hoods that could never be recovered. I grieved for the happy ending to our lives that I had imagined, perhaps once again playing cards with grandchildren at our feet or teaching them the intricate skills of playing bid whiz.

With the possibility of losing Boyce, I was losing a part of myself again, just like I had lost my leg. A part of myself was slowly being wrenched away, beyond my control to stop it. I wished we could go back to the creek again and build another dam; but just as the inevitable rain would come and wash away our mud, clay, rock, and wood dams, our diseases now were threatening to wash away our lives.

It was as if we were in a race again, like our races across the pasture or the football field, but now we both were badly wounded, stumbling and falling. Neither of us wanted to win this race toward death. I knew I at least had a fighting chance with the cancer, and I was not about to quit, but Boyce had grown tired and was fading; I did not want to be left behind.

I was receiving experimental treatment for the melanoma at the National Cancer Institute in Bethesda, Maryland, on October 28, 1997, when I heard myself being paged on the overhead speaker. I had a sense of foreboding when I heard the page because I knew that Boyce had gone to the hospital, due to a fever. I had talked to him the night before, and he had become increasingly short of breath. When I left Bethesda, I had planned to go straight back to Lincolnton to see him in the hospital. I told him I was on my way, and I told him to "hang in there." I asked him to find out who of the old crowd was around, and I suggested we might round up enough people to play cards. He seemed to be cheered up by that thought, though, at that time, he was too weak even to hold up his hands to see a card, much less play them. I figured we could have fun letting his son, B.J., help him play, and at the same time, teach B.J. some secret strategies of the game. In fact, I remember that we ended the conversation laughing.

The family doctor knew Boyce did not want to be placed on a ventilator. I had made sure that all of his wishes were carried out. Having me oversee his care seemed to be reassuring to him. He had called me often for medical advice.

When I answered the overhead page, it was my sister. She told me that Boyce had died in his sleep overnight, just a few hours after we had talked. He had stopped breathing, and true to his wishes, no efforts were made to resuscitate him, efforts which, at that point, would only have prolonged his misery.

The remainder of that day was a blur. I was filled with feelings of overwhelming sadness on one hand and, on the other, relief that his suffering and helplessness had finally ended. I slipped and fell three times that day as I made my way around the hospital finishing up my tests. I had not fallen on my artificial leg for years, but the news of Boyce's death had unnerved me. I was bitterly disappointed that I hadn't made it back in time to say goodbye to him. In a way, however, we had already said goodbye to each other many times. It was of some comfort to me to realize that Boyce had gone to sleep that night knowing I was on my way to see him and, hopefully, he was looking forward to our planned reunion game of bid whiz. I was going to miss him terribly.

I called his wife, Rita, who was in a daze. She was exhausted. The past several days had been worse than Boyce had let on to me. I told her I was heading home as fast as I could, and I asked her to call me if there was anything I could do to help her. She had already made most of the arrangements for his funeral ahead of time.

I talked briefly to B.J. I told him I was sorry his daddy had passed on, and even though he was going to miss his dad, he would always have his father inside him wherever he went, and I would always be a telephone call away if he needed anything. I don't think B.J. really understood what was happening.

It was several days before I could actually make it home to Lincolnton. Sue and I returned to Atlanta first to pick up our children so that they could attend the funeral. It was a long and depressing drive from Atlanta to Lincolnton. I spent much of it lost in thought about all the good times we had as children and teenagers, times that were now gone forever. We arrived the day before the funeral. A wake was being held in the chapel of Drum's Funeral Home. Boyce and I had graduated from high school with Steve Drum, the son of the original owner of the mortuary. Steve had long since left the family business.

I dropped my family at the old farmhouse, where my sister and her husband recently had retired. The farm had become too much for my eighty-year-old mother to manage alone. She had moved into a small apartment within walking distance of the Courthouse Square and our Lutheran Church.

I drove to the funeral home, where Boyce's body was laid out for viewing as friends and family members came and went, paying respects to Boyce, his wife, and the rest of the family. I went to the funeral home to see who was there rather than to see Boyce's body, which, to me, was only an empty shell of the spirit of the person who once dwelled there. By the time I arrived, it was late, and all of the Blakes had already gone home, except Sam. Miss Ruth was ill, "down with her back." I figured she was overwhelmed and exhausted. I would go by to see her first thing in the morning.

Sam, Boyce, and I had spent about equal time in card games, playing along the creek, and working for my father. Sam, however, regarded the farm work as more oppressive than did Boyce and I. Sam was often hard to find on Saturdays when Boyce and I would scout around looking for him to help us out with the work load.

After Sam had been drafted into the army and was sent to Vietnam, I almost lost track of him. He seemed so different from my memories of him, so much older and more serious. I figured that he had never been the same since Vietnam. At age forty-eight, his hair was already turning gray.

It was early morning before we really had time to talk. The funeral parlor had an eerie and lonely feeling. Sam and I wandered outside, where Sam could smoke. Drum's Funeral Home stood directly across the street from the Pleasant Retreat Academy that had once housed the old county library. The academy had been converted into a private museum where the Daughters, and now the Sons, of the Confederacy as well, met on a regular basis. I imagined that the ghosts of Generals Hoke and Ramseur still meandered about the place at times. On another corner of the intersection was the sheriff's department, a remodeled old grammar school, where my good friend and fellow Lutheran Church member Sheriff Barbara Pickens had told me her story of the encounter between former Sheriff Harvin Crouse and Miss Mattie.

Sam talked to me for several hours about what had happened to everybody in and around Georgetown. He seemed to know nearly everything about our childhood crowd, but he volunteered little information about himself.

Times had been hard for the Blakes in the ensuing years since Sam, Boyce, Tom, and I had finished high school.

Drafted into the army, Sam had been included in the first wave of troops that entered Cambodia in Nixon's and Kissinger's "secret war," in which American troops sought the communist troops who were using that country as sanctuary. Sam saw combat but never talked about Vietnam, not even with Boyce. For several years after returning home, he drank heavily. After a period of time, however, he straightened himself out, got a job, married, and had a number of children and even grandchildren.

Tom had voluntarily joined the air force during Vietnam, had spent most of his time on administrative duty in Saigon, then had returned home and married, as well. Out of six sons, two of the Blake brothers had served in Vietnam, and all had been discharged honorably, yet none of their children or grandchildren ever were allowed to swim in the all-white pool of the local chapter of the Veterans of Foreign Wars.

Frank had managed to avoid Vietnam, but he had gotten into a violent argument with a neighbor in Georgetown for some unknown reason and had shot and killed him. He spent a number of years in prison, was released, and had finished up his parole. He married, became a respectable member of the community, and had grandchildren. One of Frank's daughters died a few years ago of breast cancer at age thirty-three.

Johnny Blake, my good friend, bid whiz nemesis, moonshine mentor, and midnight savior, was killed in an automobile accident. He was only forty-nine years old. Johnny had remained loyal to the end. He never identified me to Johnny Farmer as the leader of the brigade of flashlight ambushers who spotlighted him with Betsy Sharpe.

Sister Peggy, who had restored order that raucous day under the apple tree, had died painfully of colon cancer only six months before Boyce's death at age forty-six. One of her sons was in college. The other was a straight-A high school student who wanted to go the University of North Carolina at Chapel Hill. Johnson Blake, the family patriarch, died at age sixty-nine in 1975, of prostate cancer in a Veterans Hospital. My own father, George, had died of stomach cancer at age sixty-three in 1982. Miss Ruth, who suffered from chronic back pain due to severe arthritis, had been recently diagnosed with colon cancer and had surgery scheduled, then postponed, due to Boyce's rapidly deteriorating health. Miss Ruth died in 1998, six months after Boyce's death.

All of the Blake sisters were married. Punkin, or Donna, as she was still called by everyone except her brothers and sisters and me, had two male Punkins herself, fine, strong, bright teenage boys, Richard and Robert. Punkin and her husband, David, had built a new house across from our farm property, only a stone's throw away from the creek where we all spent countless hours playing.

The old Blake house was torn down a number of years ago, and Blake Hill was now populated by the descendants of Johnson and Ruth Blake in newly built houses. A new church had been built on their property, and the road to Blake Hill was paved and named Johnson Blake Drive by the county. Miss Ruth, in spite of her health problems, the death of Johnson, Bob, Johnny, and Peggy, had nonetheless endured as the indomitable matriarch of the family. Miss Ruth was not overtly religious, preachy, or pious, but a better person never walked the earth, as far as I was concerned. Her quiet and strong faith and the strong support of her children sustained her through the worst of times.

Tragic events seemed to be an integral part of the life of Georgetown. Johnny Wayne Dorsey, one of my best friends and one of the card players under the apple tree that notorious day, had come home from the army one night, found his wife in bed with another man, and had shot the man dead in his front yard as he tried to escape. Johnny spent a number of years in prison, then was released on parole early for good behavior. He returned to the same house in Georgetown and eventually remarried and became a truck driver. Along with Frank Blake, Johnny Wayne became a hardworking and respected member of the few families who had chosen to remain in the slowly diminishing black enclave of Georgetown. Walter Sherrill, who lived beside Johnny Wayne in Georgetown in a tiny four-room house, had escaped

Lincolnton altogether and is currently a forensic toxicologist with the medical examiner's office in Philadelphia.

Annette Jarrett, who lived across the road from Johnny Wayne, had been one of the most beautiful girls in Georgetown, as well as at Lincolnton High School, when she joined our senior year. Annette was elected to the Homecoming Court, the only black student included, along with the Homecoming Queen Carole Cochrane, my seventh-grade sweetheart. Annette married a career military officer and has spent much of her life in Europe.

Sylvester Cansler, another hand at the table that apple-tree day, had joined the navy as a career, but died of kidney cancer at the age of forty-seven. His younger brother Linton remained in Georgetown and lived with his parents.

Sylvester Diamond, Mary Jane's brother, one of my favorite buddies of all time, and fullback on the football team, died of a bleeding ulcer, likely alcohol-induced, at age twenty-one. He had bled to death after being turned away from one of the local hospitals, where he had gone with stomach pains. He had no insurance and was probably viewed as an unlikely credit risk for the emergency room.

As for the Pratts along Victory Grove Church Road, the abuse of the family was put to an end one night when brother Jimmy put a butcher knife through his drunken father's heart in defense of his mother. The court ruling was lenient; it probably should have been declared justifiable homicide. Jimmy served a few years in prison, subsequently married, and currently has grandchildren. Johnny Farmer owns a respectable and successful car garage located behind his house on Victory Grove Church Road. I recently negotiated with Johnny over the telephone to find and rebuild a classic Ford Mustang in time for my son's sixteenth birthday.

My school-bus bodyguard, Johnny's brother Frankie, met a violent death. Apparently, Frankie was involved in a theft ring with a certain "Apache" Baumgardner from Flat Shoals, a not-too-distant neighbor of Mary Long's. They stole residential heat pumps and sold them. They were caught and arrested, but Frankie struck a deal with the district attorney. Rumor had it that Frankie had turned state's evidence and presumably revealed additional crimes involving Apache. A few weeks before the trial, Apache kicked down the door of Frankie's house and shot him dead on the spot. Solving the crime was not difficult, as it was clear to the sheriff that there was only one person who wanted Frankie dead. Apache is still in prison, as far as I know.

Moonshining in Lincoln County ended when the county voted around 1970 to have legal liquor stores operated by the state. Miss Mattie was long dead, but Sheriff Harvin Crouse was still living and well. I dropped by to see him and to reminisce about the days of patrolling Bootleg Hill near our house, racing after stock cars loaded with moonshine down the mountainous "thunder roads" of western Carolina, and hiding under Miss Mattie's house that famous night. Apparently, Miss Mattie's dog Blue had lived to a comfortable old age and, just like his master, had died peaceably in his sleep.

The bootleggers Bud Hester and Burl Plonck died years ago. Their houses had either burned or been torn down. The wild and dangerous, yet funny and colorful days of Bootleg Hill were over. That property had been bought by a local developer and was now crowned with fine homes that had, besides our farm site, the grandest view of town, as well as the front range of the South Mountains, visible in the distance. Bootleg Hill's most recent inhabitants have no idea of the raucous history of the road nor of the reprobates who once lived on the land upon which their stately homes now stand.

The Scots-Irish of the Carolinas finally won their right to buy and drink whiskey as they so chose . . . well, almost. There was still no "liquor by the drink" in any establishment in Lincoln County.

There are so many other funny and tragic stories to be told of the families and personages of the community of Georgetown. Sam knew more than I, but even he could recall only a fraction of the history of this small community that was once an enclave for newly released slaves. On the edge of Georgetown, there is a small dirt road where the county placed an official road sign that read simply and ironically, "Untold Way." I knew that I could tell but part of the tale of these people. There are countless stories of Georgetown that are lost to time and memory forever. I wanted to relate, nevertheless, what I knew of the Blake family, of their fun and suffering, and of our various adventures.

As Sam and I talked late into the night, my thoughts would drift away and connect to other memories. Mary and I gradually drifted apart after high school. She did make it to college, thanks to the money she saved by working in a cotton mill during the summer after high school and thanks to a small scholarship. We attended separate colleges only about a hundred miles apart. I felt a need to break away from her, a need that, I believe, was part of my effort to break away from my small town. I was the one who gradually became unfaithful in the long-distance romance. I began dating other girls at college, and when I told her, she seemed hurt and surprised, but not devastated. We saw nothing of each other after that conversation. I believe she wanted to let go of me, just as I was pushing her away. I think we both felt the need to build separate lives for ourselves and to leave Lincolnton and the South Fork River behind. If Mary was hurt badly by the breakup, I now realize she was not able to show it any more than she overtly showed any grief about the death of her brother. She carried the pain in her life deeply and quietly. Because she did not share many of her feelings with me, even though we had been so close as teenagers, there was a part of her that I could never completely know. When we left each other at age nineteen, she continued to cover her grief as one covers an unhealed wound.

I never even knew what her college major was or what kind of work she chose. I learned through my mother that she married a career military man and that she had lived in various parts of the country. I also learned from the few friends of hers I ran into over the years that her father had died, that her mother had remarried and moved out of state, and that she had cut all of her ties to Flat Shoals and to Lincolnton. She had never come back, even for class reunions. I figured there was little for her to come back to, except dismal memories of life in the mill, the muddy river that ran by her house, and the graves of her family.

Thinking about her brother's death, her life in the mill village in the shade of the abandoned rusty steel bridge that crossed the South Fork River and about her parents' silent, unhappy marriage, I understood better why she wanted to close the door on the past, and that past included me. I speculated over and analyzed these things about her much as I might a patient with a painful past.

I was tired of death, and I felt, like Boyce near the end of his life, I had become tired of the misery of life, and yet, in spite of all the misfortunes, I still felt that something unutterable, something like God, dwelt in this land and that there was hope to be found in these hills of home and that I might still find hope within myself. I wished to find something meaningful out of all of this suffering, both mine and Boyce's.

Sam continued to talk through my distracted thoughts, but he brought me back when I heard him say, "Zeke, we sure had some good times growing up, except having to pick up a million rocks to fill up that damned old well for your daddy!"

We both laughed. "That well!" I said, "Between you, me, and Boyce, we really must have picked up a million rocks, but I think my old man was always afraid one of us was going to fall in it. I think that's why he was so obsessed with it. My father was frightened of death. His mother died when he was only twelve years old, and I think that filling up that well was his way of doing what he could to avoid death. Or maybe he was trying to fill up some emptiness inside himself. But he couldn't avoid death, and he can't keep it from coming for us one day, just like it came for Boyce."

"Yeah," replied Sam, "that's probably what that was all about, and as much trouble as we got into around there, we probably would have fallen down that empty well before it was over with!" We laughed again.

"There's one thing I always wanted to ask you about, Sam. How come you never talked about what happened to you in Vietnam?" I surmised that, twenty-five years later, Vietnam was still eating at him like cancer seemed to be eating at me.

Sam grew quiet and seemed surprised that I had suddenly changed the subject. "I don't know, Zeke. I saw too much in 'Nam. All you had to do was to take one step in that jungle and you could see how we were never going to win that war. When we'd do the body counts after a fire fight, the Viet Cong had these loops tied on the backs of their shirts, so they could be dragged off and buried instead of being left out to rot in the sun because their bodies were too much trouble to handle either for us or for their own men. Just think of that, going to fight, forced to sew those loops on their own uniforms in case they bought it." I wondered if Sam might be launching into a long-overdue catharsis.

Sam went on. "And there was Paul Lawing. You remember Paul and how we used to play basketball together?" I nodded. "Well, Paul had his college deferment and everything and dropped out of college anyway to join the army. Some people said it was because his brother-in-law had been killed over there, but I always thought it had more to do with some woman. I think Paul was so mad he wanted to kill somebody. Well, if that's what he wanted, he sure went to the right place. He served his year and then signed up for another one, even though he could have gotten out and come home. He was a Green Beret, you know, and one day, his platoon got pinned down on a search-and-destroy patrol. He even had this dog with him he called Sandbags, who went everywhere with him. Paul thought Sandbags could smell Viet Cong in those damn tunnels and caves they'd dig to hide in. Well,

Vonetta Blake,
Boyce's Daughter

Rita with Boyce Blake

Vonetta Blake

Closed VFW Pool

BOYCE BLAKE, ALAN "ZEKE" STOUDEMIRE, AND "MISS RUTH" IN 1997

ROBERT LAHSER/THE CHARLOTTE OBSERVER

MAURICE MOORE, BOXING, KICKBOXING
AND U.S. ARMY KARATE CHAMPION

LOUISE AND GEORGE STOUDEMIRE

DR. ALAN STOUDEMIRE WITH CHILDREN ANNA AND WILL

Shirley Blake Easter in front of the Blake family's home

Donna Blake Tolliver (Punkin)

James Franklin Blake,
Boyce's Brother

ABANDONED STEEL BRIDGE OVER THE SOUTH FORK OF THE CATAWBA RIVER

BATTLE OF RAMSOUR'S MILL MARKER WITH GRINDING STONE

DR. SCOTT NORWOOD

DUKE PEELER

WALTER SHERRILL

FRANK CAUTHEN (1947-1968)
KILLED IN ACTION, VIETNAM

CAROLE COCHRANE

BECKY BURRIS

SHERIFF BARBARA PICKENS

SUE AND ALAN STOUDEMIRE

Boyce Blake

Alan Stoudemire

Dr. Alan Stoudemire

Paul was on point and drew the first fire in an ambush on his platoon. He knew his platoon was surrounded. He ordered his men to retreat and tried to call in some air support. Well, his men got pinned down. Paul kept his position to hold off the Viet Cong until his men were all out. By the time they were clear, Paul didn't have a chance. The air strike came in too late for Paul. Sandbags bought it, too. I never talk about Vietnam probably for the same reason you never talk about what it was like getting your leg cut off."

Sitting together in the early morning hour, we fell silent in thought while the dark cloaked us in deep grief. It was an eerie silence.

We began to hear the first birds of morning wake up and begin their chirping. As we sat there heavy with our mutual sadness, the birds seemed to be saying that the long night of mourning was finally over. It was then that a long, black hearse drove by us, stopped, backed up, and pulled into the parking lot of the funeral home close to the spot where we were standing.

The window slowly rolled down, and I could see the driver was Bud Warlick, the proprietor of the other large, competing funeral home in town. I knew Bud well, but found it odd for him to be up this early. The sun had yet to rise. I had not realized until then that Sam and I had talked all night. Regular time had been suspended as we relived our childhoods, the little-known histories of the people of Georgetown, and nightmares of Vietnam.

Before he could say anything, I beat him to the mark. "What are you doing up so early, Bud, checking out the competition? What's the matter? Is business dead over at your place?" I had known Bud all my life. He currently lived in one of the stately and expensive homes built on the land that had been Bootleg Hill, not far from our farm. I visited his funeral home with my wife only a few months before, but I had almost forgotten about that unusual afternoon. I had a feeling he was not going to let me forget it for long.

Bud Warlick was a distant descendant of Elizabeth Warlick Reinhardt, the wife of Christian Reinhardt, the aforementioned tanner and Fesso's owner, as well as the sister of the two Tory Warlick brothers, Nicholas and Philip, who died at the Battle of Ramsour's Mill only a mile from Drum's Funeral Home, where we now stood. The Warlick brothers' graves were marked by a huge stone marker near my old middle school.

Bud had a friendly, buoyant personality. Appearing on the surface completely unperturbed by the nature of his business, he seemed to float above death like a mist above the South Fork River. In fact, it seemed he even relished his work in some odd way. He had inherited the family undertaking business from his father, who was a good friend of my own father.

While I could analyze his lighthearted demeanor as a psychological defense against the sadness of death and the emotional pain of the bereaved with whom he routinely worked each day, I had reached the conclusion regarding his nonchalance that he was so familiar with dying, he had lost all fear of and discomfort with it. I think he looked upon the grief of the bereaved as a surgeon must look upon the surgical wound of a patient after an operation. He knew that the healing would come in time.

"Well, if it isn't ol' Alan Stoudemire!" he opened, ignoring my worn-out jokes. While I knew Bud all too well and while I was the one responsible for initiating the teasing with him, I was not sure if I could take his irreverent banter at this point. In spite of himself, beneath his light and sometimes even silly facade, his warmth and humanity were as transparent as glass. His lack of the typical undertaker's formal and somber sympathy made one believe that perhaps death was not such a terrible thing after all.

He quickly came back at me. "That's a good one about business 'being dead.' I don't think I've heard that one before. Hold on while I write it down." I should have known better than to have started any cuttin' up with Bud. In the dark hour of the morning, everything began to take on a surreal air.

"Don't bother to write it down, Bud. I'll remind you the next time I'm over at your place, provided you won't try to embalm me prematurely. What are you doing up around here anyway at this hour? Looking for bodies along the side of the road?"

Bud had turned off the motor to his hearse, which, even in the darkness, seemed to emit a strange, dark sheen. He came over to us, all perky five foot-four inches of him. "I was on my way to the hospital to pick up somebody. All my regular night drivers were tied up. This family was real anxious and wanted someone to come over right away, so I decided just to do it myself."

I looked at Sam. "Now, Sam, when Bud says he's going to pick up somebody, he doesn't just mean 'somebody' like ordinary people; he means he's really going to pick up 'some body,' as in somebody's body. Well, whoever that body was, you can be sure that they paid in advance for Bud to come out personally before sunrise to pick the body up." Most people read the obituaries with some degree of respect for the dead. Bud reads the obituary page like it was the *Wall Street Journal.*"

Bud tried to ignore me and stuck out his hand to Sam. He and Sam shook hands in the darkness, which was now beginning to lift with the gradual arrival of the morning light. "I sure am sorry about Boyce. I remember when Boyce and Stoudemire here used to play football over at the stadium. They were quite a pair."

"Yeah, that Boyce was something," Sam responded simply, backing away from Bud. Sam wasn't prepared for this kind of chatter in the face of the death of his brother. It seemed to make him uncomfortable.

Bud, in his unrelenting style, then said to Sam, "Did Stoudemire here tell you what he did to me the other day when he came by my place with his wife?"

"No, Zeke didn't say anything about that," Sam responded, obviously becoming even more uncomfortable, if not irritated, with Bud. Sam glanced over at me as if to check if I knew what Bud was talking about. I was already shaking my head and smiling, readying myself for Bud's rendition of that bizarrely funny day when Sue and I had dropped by Warlick's Funeral Home to firm up agreements I had made with Bud by phone as to funeral arrangements in the event of my death.

"Well," Bud continued as if he were warming up for a comedy routine, "here ol' Alan comes, or Zeke, like a lot of people around here used to call him, with that gal from Memphis he married. He wanted to take a tour of the caskets like he was shopping at K-Mart. Well, about the time he gets in my office, my wife Molly calls, and I say to her, 'Molly! You'll never guess who's standing right here in my office with me? I've got Alan Stoudemire here, and he looks just great!' Then Stoudemire calls out loud enough for Molly to hear him over the phone, 'Yeah, and Bud's really disappointed!' I couldn't believe he said it, but that was only the start."

The three of us broke out into laughter. Sam choked on his cigarette. Bud continued, "Okay, okay . . . , so I try to ignore that comment and take him and his wife into the display room. Well, first, he accuses me of switching all the

price labels since I knew he was coming and since I thought
he was a rich doctor. He points out a coffin to his wife
that's marked four thousand dollars, and he says, 'That one
was probably four hundred dollars before we came in here!'
Stoudemire was treating me like some crooked used car
salesman. In fact, he kicked the coffin I had recommended
to him, just like you would the tires of a new car! Then he
says he wants something really big, but cheap, of course,
because, he says, his wife wants to be buried with him like
the wives of the kings in Egypt used to do in the pyramids.
You can imagine what his poor wife must have to put up
with under normal circumstances!"

Bud was not through with me yet. I knew there was
more to come. He was not exaggerating how I had teased him
that day. Sam and I were already weak with laughter. It probably was as therapeutic to be laughing as to be crying. We
could see each other better now. The sun had risen.

"All right," said Sam, shaking his head, "give me the
rest of it."

"Well, then, after Stoudemire had the nerve to inquire
if I had any 'used models' that were cheaper and had whittled
me down to what amounted to a cheap pine box, we were out
in the office area in front of the secretaries, finishing up
some of the paperwork. Well, right there in front of them, he
puts his arm around me and pulls me real close to him. Then
he turns to his wife and says to her in front of everybody,
'Now, Honey, you remember what Bud said to us. He said

that if you get a bill for all of this, you can just tear it up. JUST TEAR IT UP AND THROW IT AWAY! Bud says he's not charging us a thing since we've been such good friends all these years. And remember what he said about helping out with the kids' college tuition. And if there's ever any questions about anything, I'm sure these ladies will vouch for what Bud just promised us."

Before we could recover, Bud had gotten back into his hearse and had started up the engine. Without saying anything more, he had pulled away. I could discern a big grin on his face. Then he was gone, leaving us alone again.

Regaining his composure, Sam put out his last cigarette without mention of Bud. "Well, I've got to get home and get some sleep before the services. You're coming, aren't you?"

"Sure, Sam. I'll be there with Sue and the kids. I think some of the players from the old football team are coming, too. I called around to check. I'll see you then. Say hello to Miss Ruth for me. I'll come by to see her later."

I walked with Sam toward his car. "I sure hate it about Boyce, Sam. I really hate it. I'll try to do something for B.J. if y'all will let me know when he needs anything."

"Don't worry about B.J., Zeke. He's got enough folks around here to look after him. And don't go worrying about old Fox, either. I bet he's shuffling cards right now with Johnny, Peggy, Bob, and Daddy for a game of bid whiz. I'll see you this afternoon."

Sam pulled away in his car, and I was alone. It was time to go back to the farm. I decided I would swing by the old football field on the way home, probably for the last time. I had no reason to go there anymore.

During the one-mile drive to the football field and school buildings that now capped the site of the Battle of Ramsour's Mill, I slipped in one of my favorite tapes, a collection of Vietnam-era songs by the Byrds. Soon I found the song I wanted. The lyrics wafted through the very early morning as I drove toward Battleground Stadium:

> From a distance
> The world looks blue and green
> And the snow-capped mountains white
> From a distance
> The ocean meets the stream
> And the eagle takes to flight
>
> > From a distance, there is harmony
> > And it echoes through the land
> > It's the voice of hope
> > It's the voice of peace
> > It's the voice of every man
>
> From a distance
> we all have enough,
> And no one is in need
> There are no guns, no bombs, no diseases
> No hungry mouths to feed

From a distance, we are all instruments
Marching in a common band
Playing songs of hope
Playing songs of peace
They're the songs of every man

God is watching us, God is watching us,
God is watching us—from a distance.

From a distance
You look like my friend
Even though we are at war.
From a distance, I can't comprehend
What all this war is for

From a distance, there is harmony
And it echoes through the land
It's the hope of hopes
It's the love of loves
It's the heart of every man.

It's the hope of hopes
It's the love of loves
It's the song of every man.

I pulled the car onto Jeb Seagle Road, which ran into the stadium. The road had been named for Jeb Seagle, whom I knew as a boy. We grew up together in the Lutheran Church. A captain and helicopter pilot in the U. S. Marine Corps, Jeb was one of seven American soldiers killed in 1983, when President Reagan had ordered an invasion of Grenada to evict Castro's army and to stop their construction of an airport there.

I visited Grenada and found the spot where Jeb's helicopter had been shot down. Jeb was thirty years old when he died.

I turned the car to drive to the top of Battleground Hill, where a few old stone monuments were scattered about, most overgrown by weeds. Nevertheless, the top of the hill offered the best view of the area. I noticed that the road had been changed to "One Way" and that I was driving in the wrong direction. Given that it was before six o'clock in the morning and the streets were completely deserted, I decided it wouldn't hurt to drive the few hundred feet the wrong way at this time of day. Who would notice and who would care?

As I rounded a small turn and arrived at the top of the hill, I was stunned to see a City of Lincolnton police car directly in my way. I was caught in the act of driving the wrong way on a one-way street. Why would any police officer be here at this time of day? I found my luck unbelievably bad, which, at this point in time, did not seem like anything unusual. I decided I would take the proactive approach, just drive right up to the officer and use the excuse that I was from out of town and lost, hence, my confusion about driving the wrong way on this one-way street. Surely, seeing my Georgia license plate, he would let me off without a ticket. I found it exceptionally odd that he was here at all.

I pulled up beside the policeman, who, I noticed, had a mustache and, peculiarly, wore sunglasses, even though the sun had scarcely shed any light yet. His window was down, and I immediately launched into my excuse about being from out of town for a funeral and being lost, throwing my myself at his mercy. He seemed to avoid looking at me, and he seemed to be ignoring my excuses. I expected his next move would be to reach for his ticket book and ask for my driver's license.

Instead, he smiled, slowly pulled off his sunglasses, and turned so I could see him fully.

"Well, if it isn't Alan Stoudemire! Where have you been?!"

I recognized that the officer was none other than Duke Peeler. Duke and I had grown up with each other from kindergarten days in the Lutheran Church. His mother was my Cub Scout den mother when I was in the seventh grade. I was as relieved as I was surprised to see him here.

"Duke! How are you doing?! I thought you really had me! I bet you enjoyed the part about my being lost and from out of town!"

We both started laughing. I managed to ask Duke, "What are you doing up here this time of the morning anyway? Meeting somebody's wife?"

Now under reasonably good control of himself, Duke became thoughtful and looked out toward the town, which lay to the southeast. "Oh, sometimes, I just like to come up here and watch the sun rise. You can't beat it. And by the way, what are you doing up here? Is Mary Long in town?"

I shook my head. "We broke up almost thirty years ago, Duke. You're a little behind on my dating life. I'm here for Boyce Blake's funeral."

The conversation fell somber. "Yeah, I heard about that. It's a real shame." He quickly changed the subject and asked about Mary. "By the way, what ever happened to Mary Long? I've lost track of her. She must have moved away."

Having tracked down Mary's address through a mutual old friend, I had written her to let her know I was sick again. She had written back a short and terse letter, which concluded, "Good luck and good bye."

I told Duke, "Yeah, she married some guy she met in college and moved away. They say she doesn't even come home for class reunions. I made the mistake of writing her awhile ago, and she wrote me back and basically told me to 'drop dead.'"

Duke laughed again. "Well, that sounds like an appropriate response. She's probably still mad at you about something. By the way, who broke up with who? Did you break up with her?"

"Duke, I can't even remember. It seems like she would have gotten over it by now, anyway."

Duke thought a second. "Well, you know how it is. Some people never get over things. Anyway, she was from Flat Shoals. You know that."

I didn't quite know what to make of his reference to her being from Flat Shoals. There was a short lull between us, which he interrupted, saying, "Well, I've got to get back to work. Tell your mother hello for me. I'll see you around, Alan."

Duke had started up his patrol car and began to ease away. Suddenly, he stopped the car, and looked back at me with a grin. "The next time you're in this part of North Carolina, boy," he called out, "pay attention to the road signs!" He turned away, obviously chuckling to himself, and soon disappeared down the one-way road in the right direction.

It was six o'clock, and within a few minutes, I was overlooking Battleground Stadium, where Boyce and I had played football together that fateful senior year. The battleground of Ramsour's Mill was covered now by a complex of public school buildings and playgrounds, erected amidst a few memorials to the combatant neighboring Tory and Patriot farmers of June 20, 1780. The largest one was dedicated to "Philip and Nicholas Warlick, Loyal Servants of the King." Toward the east, the sky was turning pink and gold. I knew that I needed to get home soon and help my family get ready for Boyce's "Home-Going," as his church euphemistically called their funerals. Revived by the black churches, the term reflected an ancient belief that each person contained a divine spirit that was liberated at death to return home to God. I needed to go by and speak with Miss Ruth before Fox's Home-Going service. It was going to be a long day.

In the field below me, there was a memorial marker with an inscription on it that I knew by heart: "In Memory of Paul Lawing, Sergeant, United States Army Special Forces, Vietnam, May 14, 1950–June 14, 1972." This was a spirit-haunted place. There was, however, no marker in memory of the black and white compatriots from long-ago, Fesso and Adam Reep.

I gazed over the field and the river that ran by it. I could not fully imagine how all of the ancestors of Boyce, of Mary, and of my own were strangely tied together on this land nestled in the foothills of the Carolinas by the banks of Clark's Creek and the South Fork of the Catawba River. I visualized Fesso stealthily slipping through the nearby brush and woods to meet Reep so that he might relay information about the enemy Tories; Boyce's great-uncle, the Reverend Hilliard Blake, crossing from the adjacent county the now rusting and abandoned bridge over the South Fork River at Flat Shoals to assume his duties at his new African Methodist Episcopal Church in Lincolnton; Mary Long living in the shadow of that old steel bridge that led to and away from the mill village, the village of sadness from which she had wanted to escape. Then the best memory I had of the place came to mind: Boyce crossing the goal line to score the winning touchdown the night after the Klan rally and holding the ball high above his head as he was smothered in an exuberant expression of joy by both black and white members of our team.

So many lives were bound together here by the land and its forgotten people, lost in memory, thought, and time. The sun slowly rose over the Carolina hills and cast a golden glow of hope that a new day had arrived. It was time for me to go home.

About the Author

Alan Stoudemire, MD, was a Professor of Psychiatry at Emory University School of Medicine in Atlanta, Georgia. He was a Morehead Scholar at the University of North Carolina at Chapel Hill, where he graduated *cum laude* in religion. He attended medical school at the same institution and completed his medical internship and residency in psychiatry at the University of Colorado. He was a member of the Department of Psychiatry at Duke University School of Medicine until moving to Emory University School of Medicine in 1983.

Dr. Stoudemire was best known professionally for developing the concept of combined medical-psychiatric treatment programs to care for patients with medical, neurological and surgical disorders that are complicated by psychological and emotional factors.

His textbook *Psychiatric Care of the Medical Patient* is recognized internationally as the standard reference source in the field. He was also editor of two leading textbooks in psychiatric education *Human Behavior for Medical Students* and *Clinical Psychiatry for Medical Students*. Dr. Stoudemire authored over two hundred articles in the scientific literature regarding the relationship between medicine and psychiatry, and his research on the effects of depression on memory has been funded by the National Institutes of Health. He was awarded two of the highest awards in American psychiatry, the Hackett Award from the Academy of Psychosomatic Medicine and the Vestermark Award from the American Psychiatric Association.

Dr. Stoudemire edited and reprinted *Chimes of Freedom: Foundations of the American Character,* a book originally published in 1911 under the title of *An American Bible.*

In 1998, the Alan Stoudemire, M.D., Psychosocial Fund was established in his honor at the AFLAC Cancer Center as part of Children's Healthcare of Atlanta, as well as the Alan Stoudemire, M.D., Library at Egleston Children's Hospital at Emory University, in Atlanta.

Dr. Stoudemire died on February 2, 2000. He is survived by his widow, Sue Joyner Sprunt Stoudemire, and his two children, Anna Louise Stoudemire and William Sprunt Stoudemire.